Edward Wilmot Blyden, Henry M Schieffelin

The People of Africa

A series of papers on their character, condition, and future prospects. Vol. 1

Edward Wilmot Blyden, Henry M Schieffelin

The People of Africa
A series of papers on their character, condition, and future prospects. Vol. 1

ISBN/EAN: 9783337309046

Printed in Europe, USA, Canada, Australia, Japan

Cover: Foto ©Suzi / pixelio.de

More available books at **www.hansebooks.com**

THE PEOPLE OF AFRICA.

A

SERIES OF PAPERS
ON THEIR CHARACTER, CONDITION, AND FUTURE PROSPECTS

BY

E. W. BLYDEN, D.D., TAYLER LEWIS, D.D.
THEODORE DWIGHT, Esq.
ETC., ETC.

New York
ANSON D. F. RANDOLPH & CO.
1871.

CONTENTS.

THE PEOPLE OF AFRICA.

I.

THE NEGRO IN ANCIENT HISTORY.[1]

BY REV. EDWARD W. BLYDEN,

PROFESSOR OF LANGUAGES, ETC., IN LIBERIA COLLEGE.

From the Methodist Quarterly Review, January, 1869.

PRESUMING that no believer in the Bible will admit that the negro had his origin at the head waters of the Nile, on the banks of the Gambia, or in the neighborhood of the Zaire, we should like to inquire by what chasm is he separated from other descendants of Noah, who originated the great works of antiquity, so that with any truth it can be said that "if all that negroes of all generations have ever done were to be obliterated from recollection forever, the world would lose no great truth, no profitable art, no exemplary form of life. The loss of all that is African would offer no memorable deduction from anything but the

[1] This is, so far as we know, the first article in any Quarterly written by a hand claiming a pure Ethiopic lineage. The writer was born in the Island of St. Thomas, August 3, 1832, and is now thirty-nine years old. In 1845 he joined a Bible-class taught by Rev. John P. Knox, Pastor of the Reformed Dutch Church in St. Thomas, under whose ministry he united with the church, and from that time

1

earth's black catalogue of crimes."¹   In singular contrast with the disparaging statements of the naval

looked forward to the Gospel ministry. On the return to the United States of Mr. and Mrs. Knox, in 1850, they brought the young man with them for a collegiate and theological education. Public sentiment was such as to deny him admission to our colleges, and he was about to return to the West Indies disappointed, when he received an offer from the New York State Colonization Society of a free passage to Liberia, and an education in the Alexander High School. A letter from Mrs. Knox, manifesting a deep interest in his welfare, and urging him to accept the offer and devote his life to perishing Africa, decided his doubts ; and embarking in the Liberia Packet from Baltimore, he landed in Liberia, January, 1851.

He was soon accepted by the Presbyterian Missionary Board as a student for the ministry in the Alexander High School at Monrovia, then taught by Rev. D. A. Wilson, under whose tuition he rapidly became proficient in Latin and Greek as well as Geography and Mathematics. The Hebrew language not being embraced in the course of studies in the Alexander High School, he took up the study of it himself, and devoted for some time all his leisure hours to it, being anxious to read the entire Scriptures in the original languages, and especially those passages in the Old Testament which have reference to the African race.

In 1858 the Presbytery of West Africa, after the usual examination, licensed and ordained him to the Gospel ministry ; and the health of Rev. Mr. Wilson requiring him to return to the United States, Blyden was made principal of the institution as his successor, which position he held till in 1861 he was elected Professor of Greek and Latin in the Liberia College, on the Fulton Professorship, held in trust by the New York State Colonization Society.

In his early life he had acquired the colloquial use of the Spanish and Dutch languages, to which he has since added French, German, and Arabic. To this latter his attention was called by occasional intercourse with merchants from the interior of the Mandingo and other Mohammedan Negro nations, among whom the Koran is taught everywhere, and then becomes the medium of communica-

¹ Commander Foote, "Africa and the American Flag," p. 207.

officer, Volney, the great French Oriental traveller and distinguished linguist, after visiting the wonders of Egypt and Ethiopia, exclaims, as if in mournful indignation, "How are we astonished when we reflect that to the race of negroes, at present our slaves, and the objects of our extreme contempt, we owe our arts and sciences, and even the very use of speech!" And we do not see how, with the records of the past accessible to us, it is possible to escape from the conclusions of Volney. If it cannot be shown that the negro race was separated by a wide and unapproachable interval from the founders of Babylon and Nineveh, the builders of Babel and the Pyramids, then we claim for them a participation in those ancient works of science and art, and that not merely on the indefinite ground of a common humanity, but on the ground of close and direct relationship.

Let us turn to the tenth chapter of Genesis, and consider the ethnographic allusions therein contained, receiving them in their own grand and catholic spirit. And we the more readily make our appeal to this remarkable portion of Holy Writ because it has "extorted the admiration of modern ethnologists, who

tion by the educated travellers of different nations. Having made some progress in Arabic from books, and desiring to become more perfect in it, and especially to acquire a correct colloquial use of it, he in 1866 visited Syria and Beyrout College for this purpose.

During his three months' sojourn in that vicinity, he was made the orator of the day at a Fourth of July meeting of the Americans —travellers and missionaries gathered on Mount Lebanon.

The article in this volume on *Mohammedanism in Western Africa*, reprinted from the same Quarterly Review, is also from his pen.

H. M. S.

continually find in it anticipations of their greatest discoveries." Sir Henry Rawlinson says of this chapter: "The Toldoth Beni Noah (the Hebrew title of the chapter) is undoubtedly *the most authentic* record we possess for the affiliation of those branches of the human race which sprang from the triple stock of the Noachidæ." And again: "We must be cautious in drawing direct ethnological inferences from the linguistic indications of a very early age. It would be far *safer*, at any rate, in these early times, to follow the general scheme of ethnic affiliation which is given in the tenth chapter of Genesis." [1]

From the second to the fifth verse of this chapter we have the account of the descendants of Japheth and their places of residence, but we are told nothing of their *doings* or their *productions*. From the twenty-first verse to the end of the chapter we have the account of the descendants of Shem and of their "dwelling." Nothing is said of their *works*. But how different the account of the descendants of Cush, the eldest son of Ham, contained from the seventh to the twelfth verse. We read: "And Cush begat Nimrod: he began to be a mighty one in the earth. He was a mighty hunter before the Lord. . . . And the beginning of his kingdom was Babel, and Erech, and Accad, and Calneh, in the land of Shinar. Out of that land he went forth into Asshur, (marginal reading,) and builded Nineveh, and the city Rehoboth, and Calah, and Resen between Nineveh and Calah: the same is a great city."

We have adopted the marginal reading in our En-

[1] Quoted by G. Rawlinson in Notes to "Bampton Lectures," 1859.

glish Bible, which represents Nimrod as having founded Nineveh, in addition to the other great works which he executed. This reading is supported by authorities, both Jewish and Christian, which cannot be set aside. The author of "Foundations of History," without, perhaps, a due consideration of the original, affirms that Asshur was "one of the sons of Shem!" thus despoiling the descendants of Ham of the glory of having "builded" Nineveh. And to confirm this view he tells us that "Micah speaks of the land of Asshur and the land of Nimrod as distinct countries." We have searched in vain for the passage in which the Prophet makes such a representation. The verse to which this author directs us (Micah v. 6) is unfortunate for this theory. It is plain from the closing of the verse that the conjunction "*and,*" in the first clause, is not the simple copulative *and* or *also,* but is employed, according to a well-known Hebrew usage, in the sense of *even* or *namely,* to introduce the words "land of Nimrod" as an explanatory or qualifying addition in apposition to the preceding "land of Assyria."[1]

We must take Asshur in Gen. x. 11, not as the subject of the verb "went," but as the name of the place whither—the *terminus ad quem.* So Drs. Smith and Van Dyck, eminent Oriental scholars, understand the passage, and so they have rendered it in their admirable Arabic translation of the Bible, recently adopted by the British and Foreign Bible Society, namely, "Out of that land he (Nimrod) went forth unto Asshur

[1] See Conant's Gesenius's Hebrew Grammar, (17th edition,) section 155, (a) ; and for additional examples of this usage see Judges vii. 22 ; 1 Sam. xvii. 40 ; Jer. xv. 13, where *even* represents the conjunction *vau* (and) in the original.

—Assyria—and builded Nineveh." De Sola, Linden-
thal, and Raphall, learned Jews, so translate the passage in their "New Translation of the Book of Genesis."[1] Dr. Kalisch, another Hebrew of the Hebrews,
so renders the verse in his "Historical and Critical
Commentary on Genesis."[2] All these authorities, and
others we might mention, agree that to make the passage descriptive of the Shemite Asshur is to do
violence to the passage itself and its context. Asshur,
moreover, is mentioned in his proper place in verse 22,
and without the least indication of an intention of describing him as the founder of a rival empire to Nimrod.[3] Says Nachmanides, (quoted by De Sola, etc.):
"It would be strange if Asshur, a son of Shem, were
mentioned among the descendants of Ham of whom
Nimrod was one. It would be equally strange if the
deeds of Asshur were spoken of before his birth and
descent had been mentioned."

The grammatical objection to our view is satisfac-
torily disposed of by Kalisch.[4] On the absence of
the *(he)* locale he remarks: "The *(he)* locale, after
verbs of motion, though frequently, is by no means
uniformly, applied. (1 Kings xi. 17; 2 Kings xv. 14;
etc.) Gesenius, whose authority no one will dispute,
also admits the probability of the view we have taken,
without raising any objection of grammatical structure."

[1] London, 1844.
[2] London, 1858. See Dr. Robinson's view in Gesenius's Hebrew
Lexicon, under the word Cush.
[3] See Kitto's Biblical Cyclopedia, article, *Ham.* London, 1866.
[4] Historical and Critical Commentary on Genesis. Heb. and Eng.
P. 263.

But enough on this point. We may reasonably suppose that the building of the *tower of Babel* was also the work, principally, of Cushites. For we read in the tenth verse that Nimrod's kingdom was in the land of Shinar ; and in the second verse of the eleventh chapter we are told that the people who undertook the building of the tower, "found a plain in the land of *Shinar*" which they considered suitable for the ambitious structure. And, no doubt, in the "scattering" which resulted, these sons of Ham found their way into Egypt,[1] where their descendants—inheriting the skill of their fathers, and guided by tradition—erected the pyramids in imitation of the celebrated tower. Herodotus says that the tower was six hundred and sixty feet high, or one hundred and seventy feet higher than the great pyramid of Cheops. It consisted of eight square towers one above another. The winding path is said to have been four miles in length. Strabo calls it a pyramid.

But it may be said, The enterprising people who founded Babylon and Nineveh, settled Egypt and built the Pyramids, though descendants of Ham, were not *black*—were not negroes; for, granted that the negro race have descended from Ham, yet, when these great civilizing works were going on the descendants of Ham had not yet reached that portion of Africa, had not come in contact with those conditions of climate and

---

[1] It is certain that Mizraim, with his descendants, settled Egypt, giving his name to the country, which it still retains. The Arabic name for Egypt is *Misr*. In Psalm cv. 23, Egypt is called "the land of Ham."

atmosphere which have produced that peculiar development of humanity known as the Negro.

' Well, let us see. It is not to be doubted that from the earliest ages the black complexion of some of the descendants of Noah was known. Ham, it would seem, was of a complexion darker than that of his brothers. The root of the name Ham, in Hebrew, *Hamam*, conveys the idea of *hot* or *swarthy*. So the Greeks called the descendants of Ham, from their black complexion, *Ethiopians*, a word signifying *burnt* or *black* face. The Hebrews called them Cushites, a word probably of kindred meaning. Moses is said to have married a Cushite or Ethiopian woman, that is, a *black* woman descended from Cush. The query, " Can the Ethiopian change his skin ?" seems to be decisive as to a difference of complexion between the Ethiopian and the Shemite, and the etymology of the word itself determines that the complexion of the former was black. The idea has been thrown out that the three principal colors now in the world—white, brown, and black—were represented in the ark in Japheth, Shem, and Ham.

But were these enterprising descendants of Ham *woolly-haired?*—a peculiarity that, in these days, seems to be considered a characteristic mark of degradation and servility.[1] On this point let us consult Herodotus,

[1] While Rev. Elias Schrenk, a German missionary laboring on the Gold Coast, in giving evidence on the condition of West Africa before a committee of the House of Commons in May, 1865, was making a statement of the proficiency of some of the natives in his school in Greek and other branches of literature, he was interrupted by Mr. Cheetham, a member of the committee, with the inquiry : "Were those young men of *pure* African blood?" "Yes, '

called " the father of history." He lived nearly three
thousand years ago. Having travelled extensively in
Egypt and the neighboring countries, he wrote from
personal observation. His testimony is that of an
eye-witness. He tells us that there were two divisions
of Ethiopians, who did not differ at all from each
other in appearance, except in their language and
hair; "for the eastern Ethiopians," he says, "are
straight-haired, but those of Libya (or Africa) have
hair more curly than that of any other people."[1] He
records also the following passage, which fixes the
physical characteristics of the Egyptians and some of
their mighty neighbors :[2]

The Colchians were evidently Egyptians, and I say this, *having myself observed it* before I heard it from others ; and as it
was a matter of interest to me, I *inquired* of both people, and
the Colchians had more recollection of the Egyptians than the
Egyptians had of the Colchians ; yet the Egyptians said that
they thought the Colchians had descended from the army of
Sesostris ; and I formed my conjecture, *not only because they
are black in complexion and woolly-haired*, for this amounts to
nothing, because *others are so likewise*, etc., etc.[3]

Rawlinson has clearly shown[4] that these statements

replied Mr. Schrenk, "decidedly ; thick lips and black skin."
"And woolly hair?" added Mr. Cheetham. "And woolly hair,"
subjoined Mr. Schrenk. (See "Parliamentary Report on Western
Africa for 1865," p. 145.)

[1] Herodotus, iii. 94 ; vii. 70.

[2] It is not necessary, however, to consider *all* Egyptians as negroes, black in complexion and woolly-haired ; this is contradicted
by their mummies and portraits. Blumenbach discovered three
varieties of physiognomy on the Egyptian paintings and sculptures ;
but he describes the general or national type as exhibiting a certain
approximation to the Negro.

[3] Herodotus, ii. 104.   [4] Five Great Monarchies, vol. i. chap. 3.

1*

of Herodotus have been too strongly confirmed by all
recent researches (among the cuneiform inscriptions)
in comparative philology to be set aside by the totter-
ing criticism of such superficial inquirers as the Notts
and Gliddons, *et id omne genus*, who base their
assertions on ingenious conjectures. Pindar and
Æschylus corroborate the assertions of Herodotus.

Homer, who lived still earlier than Herodotus, and
who had also travelled in Egypt, makes frequent
mention of the Ethiopians. He bears the same
testimony as Herodotus as to their division into two
sections :

Αἰϑίοπας, τοὶ διχϑὰ δεδαίαται, ἔσχατοι ἀνδρῶν,
Ὁι μὲν δυσομένου Ὑπερίονος, οἱ δ᾽ ἀνιόντος—[1]

which Pope freely renders :

"A race divided, whom with sloping rays
The rising and descending sun surveys."

And Homer seems to have entertained the very highest opinion of these Ethiopians. It would appear that
he was so struck with the wonderful works of these
people, which he saw in Egypt and the surrounding
country, that he raises their authors above mortals,
and makes them associates of the gods. Jupiter, and
sometimes the whole Olympian family with him, is
often made to betake himself to Ethiopia to hold converse with and partake of the hospitality of the Ethiopians.[1]

But it may be asked, Are we to suppose that the
Guinea negro, with all his peculiarities, is descended
from these people? We answer, Yes. The descend-

[1] Odyssey, i, 23, 24.　　　　　　[2] Iliad, i. 423 ; xxiii. 206.

ants of Ham, in those early ages, like the European
nations of the present day, made extensive migrations
and conquests. They occupied a portion of two
continents. While the Shemites had but little connection with Africa, the descendants of Ham, on the
contrary, beginning their operations in Asia, spread
westward and southward, so that as early as the time
of Homer they had not only occupied the northern
portions of Africa, but had crossed the great desert,
penetrated into Soudan, and made their way to the
west coast. "As far as we know," says that distinguished Homeric scholar, Mr. Gladstone, " Homer
recognized the African coast by placing the Lotophagi
upon it, and the *Ethiopians inland from the East all
the way to the* extreme West." [1]

Some time ago Professor Owen, of the New York
Free Academy, well known for his remarkable accuracy in editing the ancient classics, solicited the
opinion of Professor Lewis of the New York University, another eminent scholar, as to the localities
to which Homer's Ethiopians ought to be assigned.
Professor Lewis gave a reply which so pleased Professor Owen that he gives it entire in his notes on the
Odyssey, as "the most rational and veritable com-
ment of any he had met with." It is as follows :

I have always, in commenting on the passage to which you
refer, explained it to my classes as denoting the black race,
(or Ethiopians, as they were called in Homer's time,) living
on the eastern and western coast of Africa—the one class in-
habiting the country now called Abyssinia, and the other that
part of Africa called Guinea or the Slave Coast. The com-

[1] "Homer and the Homeric Age," vol. iii. p. 305.

mon explanation that it refers to two divisions of Upper
Egypt separated by the Nile, besides, as I believe, being
geographically incorrect, (the Nile really making no such
division,) does not seem to be of sufficient importance to
warrant the strong expressions of the text. (Odyssey, i. 22-24.)
If it be said the view I have taken supposes too great a knowledge of geography in Homer, we need only bear in mind that
he had undoubtedly visited Tyre, where the existence of the
black race on the West of Africa had been known from the
earliest times. The Tyrians, in their long voyages, having
discovered a race on the West, in almost every respect similar
to those better known in the East, would, from their remote
distance from each other, and not knowing of any intervening
nations in Africa, naturally style them the two extremities of
the earth. (Homer's εσχατοι ανδρων.) Homer elsewhere
speaks of the Pigmies, who are described by Herodotus and
Diodorus Siculus as residing in the interior of Africa, (on a
river which I think corresponds to what is now called the
Niger.) It seems to me too extravagant language, even for
poetry, to represent two nations, separated only by a river, as
living, one at the rising, the other at the setting sun, although
these terms may sometimes be used for East and West. Besides, if I am not mistaken, no such division is recognized in
subsequent geography.[1]

Professor Lewis says nothing of the *Asiatic* division
of the Ethiopians. But since his letter was penned—
more than twenty years ago—floods of light have been
thrown upon the subject of Oriental antiquities by the
labors of M. Botta, Layard, Rawlinson, Hinks, and
others. Even Bunsen, not very long ago, declared
that "the idea of an '*Asiatic Cush*' was an imagination of interpreters, the child of despair." But in
1858, Sir Henry Rawlinson having obtained a number
of Babylonian documents more ancient than any pre-

[1] Owen's Homer's Odyssey, (Fifth Edition,) p. 306.

viously discovered, was able to declare authoritatively that the early inhabitants of South Babylonia *were of a cognate race with the primitive colonists both of Arabia and of the African Ethiopia.*[1] He found their *vocabulary to be undoubtedly Cushite or Ethiopian,* belonging to that stock of tongues which in the sequel were everywhere more or less mixed up with the Semitic languages, but of which we have the purest modern specimens in the " Mahra of Southern Arabia," and the " Galla of Abyssinia." He also produced evidence of the widely-spread settlements of the children of Ham *in Asia as well as Africa,* and (what is more especially valuable in our present inquiry) of the truth of the tenth chapter of Genesis as an ethnographical document of the highest importance.[1]

Now, we should like to ask, If the negroes found at this moment along the West and East coast, and throughout Central Africa, are not descended from the ancient Ethiopians, from whom are they descended? And if they are the children of the Ethiopians, what is the force of the assertions continually repeated, by even professed friends of the negro, that the enterprising and good-looking tribes of the continent, such as Lalofs, Mandingoes, and Foulahs, are mixed with the blood of Caucasians?[3] With the records of ancient history before us, where is the necessity for supposing such an admixture? May not the intelligence, the activity, the elegant features and limbs of

[1] Rawlinson's Herodotus. Vol. i. p. 442.
[2] See Article *Ham,* in Kitto's Cyclopedia. Last Edition.
[3] Bowen's " Central Africa," chap. xxii.

these tribes have been directly transmitted from their ancestors?

The Foulahs have a tradition that they are the descendants of Phut, the son of Ham. Whether this tradition be true or not, it is a singular fact that they have prefixed this name to almost every district of any extent which they have ever occupied. They have Futa-Torro, near Senegal ; Futa-Bondu and Futa-Iallon to the north-east of Sierra Leone.[1]

Lenormant was of the opinion that Phut peopled Libya.

We gather from the ancient writers already quoted that the Ethiopians were celebrated for their beauty. Herodotus speaks of them as "men of large stature, *very handsome* and long-lived." And he uses these epithets in connection with the Ethiopians of *West Africa*, as the context shows. The whole passage is as follows :

Where the meridian declines toward the setting sun (that is, south-west from Greece) the Ethiopian territory reaches, being the extreme part of the habitable world. It produces much gold, huge elephants, wild trees of all kinds, *ebony*, and men of large stature, *very handsome*, and long-lived.[2]

Homer frequently tells us of the "handsome Ethiopians," although he and Herodotus do not employ the same Greek word. In Herodotus the word that describes the Ethiopians is καλος—a word denoting both beauty of outward form and moral beauty, or virtue.[3] The epithet (αμυμων) employed by Homer to describe the same people, is by some commentators rendered "blameless," but by the generality "hand-

---

[1] Wilson's Western Africa, p. 79.   [2] Herodotus, iii. 114.
[3] Liddell and Scott.

some." Anthon says : "It is an epithet given to all men and women distinguished by rank, exploits, or beauty."[1] Mr. Hayman, one of the latest and most industrious editors of Homer, has in one of his notes the following explanation : *'Αμυμων* was at first an epithet of distinctive excellence, but had become a purely conventional style, as applied to a class, like our 'honorable and gallant gentleman.'"[2] Most scholars, however, agree with Mr. Paley, another recent Homeric commentator, that the original signification of the word was "handsome," and that it nearly represented the *καλος καγαϑος* of the Greeks ;[3] so that the words which Homer puts into the mouth of Thetis when addressing her disconsolate son (Iliad, i. 423) would be, "Yesterday Jupiter went to Oceanus, to the *handsome* Ethiopians, to a banquet, and with him went all the gods." It is remarkable that the Chaldee, according to Bush, has the following translation of Numbers xii. 1 : "And Miriam and Aaron spake against Moses because of the beautiful woman whom he had married ; for he had married a beautiful woman."[4] Compare with this Solomon's declaration, "I am *black* but *comely*," or, more exactly, "I am black *and* comely." We see the wise man in his spiritual epithalamium selecting a black woman as a proper representative of the Church and of the highest purity. The Hebrew word, translated in our version *black*, is a correct rendering. So Luther, *schwarz*. It cannot mean *brown*, as rendered by Ostervald (*brune*) and Diodati (*bruna*.) In Lev.

[1] Anthon's Homer, p. 491. [2] Hayman's Odyssey, i. 29.
[3] Paley's Iliad, p. 215. Note. [4] Bush, *in loco*.

xiii. 31, 37, it is applied to hair. The verb from
which the adjective comes is used (Job xxx. 30) of
the countenance blackened by disease. In Solomon's
Song, v. 11, it is applied to the plumage of a raven.[1]
In the days of Solomon, therefore, black, as a physical
attribute, was *comely*.

But when, in the course of ages, the Ethiopians had
wandered into the central and southern regions of
Africa, encountering a change of climate and altered
character of food and modes of living, they fell into
intellectual and physical degradation. This degradation did not consist, however, in a change of color, as
some suppose, for they were black, as we have seen,
before they left their original seat. Nor did it consist
in the stiffening and shortening of the hair; for Herodotus tells us that the Ethiopians in Asia were *straight-
haired*, while their relatives in Africa, from the same
stock and in no lower stage of progress, were *woolly-
haired*. The hair, then, is not a fundamental characteristic, nor a mark of degradation. Some suppose
that the hair of the negro is affected by some peculiarity in the African climate and atmosphere—perhaps
the influence of the Sahara entering as an important
element. We do not profess to know the *fons et
origo*, nor have we seen any satisfactory cause for it
assigned. We have no consciousness of any inconvenience from it, except that in foreign countries, as a

[1] A correspondent of the New York Tribune, residing in Syria,
describing the appearance of a negro whom he met there in 1866,
says : "He was as *black* as a Mount Lebanon raven." (N. Y.
Tribune, October 16, 1866.) Had he been writing in Hebrew he
would have employed the descriptive word שָׁחֹר

jovial fellow-passenger on an English steamer once reminded us, "it is *unpopular*."

"Vuolsi così colà, dove si puote
Ciò che si vuole : e più non dimandare." [1]

Nor should it be thought strange that the Ethiopians who penetrated into the heart of the African continent should have degenerated, when we consider their distance and isolation from the quickening influence of the arts and sciences in the East; their belief, brought with them, in the most abominable idolatry, "changing the glory of the incorruptible God into an image made like unto corruptible man, and to *birds*, and *four-footed beasts*, and *creeping things*," Rom. i. 23 ; the ease with which, in the prolific regions to which they had come, they could secure the means of subsistence ; and the constant and enervating heat of the climate, indisposing to continuous exertion. Students in natural history tell us that animals of the same species and family, if dispersed and domesticated, show striking modifications of the original type, in their color, hair, integument, structure of limbs, and even in their instincts, habits, and powers. Similar changes are witnessed among mankind. An intelligent writer in No. 48 of the "Dublin University Magazine," says :

There are certain districts in Leitrim, Sligo, and Mayo, chiefly inhabited by the descendants of the native Irish, driven by the British from Armagh and the South of Down about two centuries ago. These people, whose ancestors were well-grown, able-bodied, and comely, are now reduced to an average stature of five feet two inches, are pot-bellied, bow-legged, and abortively featured : and they are especially remarkable

[1] Dante.

for open projecting mouths, and prominent teeth, and exposed gums, their advancing cheek-bones and depressed noses bearing barbarism in their very front. In other words, within so short a period, they seem to have acquired a prognathous type of skull, like the Australian savages.

But these retrogressive changes are taking place in other countries besides Ireland. Acute observers tell us that in England, the abode of the highest civilization of modern times, " a process of de-civilization, a relapse toward barbarism, is seen in the debased and degraded classes, with a coincident deterioration of physical type." Mr. Henry Mayhew, in his " London Labor and London Poor," has remarked that

Among them, according as they partake more or less of the pure vagabond nature, doing nothing whatever for their living, but moving from place to place, preying on the earnings of the more industrious portion of the community, so will the attributes of the nomadic races be found more or less marked in them ; and they are more or less distinguished by their high cheek-bones and protruding jaws ; thus showing that kind of mixture of the pyramidal with the prognathous type which is to be seen among the most degraded of the Malayo-Polynesian races.

In contrast with this retrogressive process, it may be observed that in proportion as the degraded races are intellectually and morally elevated, their physical appearance improves. Mr. C. S. Roundell, Secretary to the late Royal Commission in Jamaica, tells us that

The Maroons who fell under my (his) own observation in Jamaica, exhibited a marked superiority in respect of comportment, mental capacity, and physical type—a superiority to be referred to the saving effects of long-enjoyed freedom. The

Maroons are descendants of runaway Spanish slaves, who at the time of the British conquest established themselves in the mountain fastnesses.[1]

In visiting the native towns interior to Liberia, we have seen striking illustrations of these principles. Among the inhabitants of those towns we could invariably distinguish the free man from the slave. There was about the former a dignity of appearance, an openness of countenance, an independence of air, a firmness of step, which indicated the absence of oppression; while in the latter there was a depression of countenance, a general deformity of appearance, an awkwardness of gait, which seemed to say, "That man is a slave."

Now, with these well-known principles before us, why should it be considered strange that, with their fall into barbarism, the "handsome" Ethiopians of Homer and Herodotus should have deteriorated in physical type—and that this degradation of type should continue reproducing itself in the wilds of Africa and in the Western Hemisphere, where they have been subjected to slavery and various other forms of debasing proscription?

*Ἥμισυ γάρ τ' ἀρετῆς ἀποαίνυται εὐρύοπα Ζεύς
Ἀνέρος, εὖτ' ἄν μιν κατὰ δούλιον ἦμαρ ἔλῃσιν.*[2]

The Negro is often taunted by superficial investigators with proofs, as is alleged, taken from the monuments of Egypt, of the servitude of Negroes in very

---

[1] "England and her Subject Races, with special reference to Jamaica." By Charles Saville Roundell, M. A.
[2] Odyssey, xvii. 322, 323.

remote ages. But is there anything singular in the
fact that in very early times Negroes were held in
bondage? Was it not the practice among all the
early nations to enslave each other? Why should it
be pointed to as an exceptional thing that Ethiopians
were represented as slaves? It was very natural that
the more powerful Ethiopians should seize upon the
weaker, as is done to this day in certain portions of
Africa, and reduce them to slavery. And were it not
for the abounding light of Christianity now enjoyed in
Europe, the same thing would be done at this moment
in Rome, Paris, and London. For the sites of those
cities in ancient times witnessed all the horrors of a
cruel and mercenary slave-trade, not in Negroes, but
Caucasian selling Caucasian.[1]

But were there no Caucasian slaves in Egypt? If
it be true that no such slaves are represented on the
monumental remains, are we, therefore, to infer that
they did not exist in that country? Are we to disbe-
lieve that the Jews were in the most rigorous bondage
in that land for four hundred years?

[1] Cicero, in one of his letters, speaking of the success of an expedition against Britain, says the only plunder to be found consisted
"Ex emancipiis ; ex quibus nullos puto te literis aut musicis erudi-
tos expectare ;" thus proving, in the same sentence, the existence of
the slave trade, and intimating that it was impossible that any
Briton should be intelligent enough to be worthy to serve the accomplished Atticus. (Ad. Att., lib. iv. 16.) Henry, in his History
of England, gives us also the authority of Strabo for the prevalence
of the slave trade among the Britons, and tells us that slaves were
once an established article of export. "Great numbers," says he,
"were exported from Britain, and were to be seen exposed for sale,
like cattle, in the Roman market."—*Henry*, vol. ii. p. 225. Also,
Sir T. Fowell Buxton's "Slave Trade and Remedy"—*Introduction*.

Not every thing which is not represented on the monuments was therefore necessarily unknown to the Egyptians. The monuments are neither intended to furnish, nor can they furnish, a complete delineation of all the branches of public and private life, of all the products and phenomena of the whole animal, vegetable, and mineral creations of the country. They cannot be viewed as a complete cyclopædia of Egyptian customs and civilization. Thus we find no representation of fowls and pigeons, although the country abounded in them ; of the wild ass and wild boar, although frequently met with in Egypt ; none of the process relating to the casting of statues and other objects in bronze, although many similar subjects connected with the arts are represented ; none of the marriage ceremony, and of numerous other subjects.[1]

But we are told that the Negroes of Central and West Africa have proved themselves essentially inferior, from the fact, that in the long period of three thousand years they have shown no signs of progress. In their country, it is alleged, are to be found no indications of architectural taste or skill, or of any susceptibility of æsthetic or artistic improvement; that they have no monuments of past exploits ; no paintings or sculptures ; and that, therefore, the foreign or American slave-trade was an indispensable agency in the civilization of Africa ; that nothing could have been done for the Negro while he remained in his own land, bound to the practices of ages ; that he needed the sudden and violent severance from home to deliver him from the quiescent degradation and stagnant barbarism of his ancestors ; that otherwise the civilization of Europe could never have impressed him.

In reply to all this we remark : 1st, That it remains to be proved, by a fuller explanation of the interior,

[1] Dr. Kalisch : "Commentary on Exodus," p. 147. London, 1855.

that there are no architectural remains, no works of
artistic skill; 2dly, If it should be demonstrated that
nothing of the kind exists, this would not necessarily
prove essential inferiority on the part of the African.
What did the Jews produce in all the long period of
their history before and after their bondage to the
Egyptians, among whom, it might be supposed, they
would have made some progress in science and art?
Their forefathers dwelt in tents before their Egyptian
residence, and they dwelt in tents after their emanci-
pation. And in all their long national history they
produced no remarkable architectural monument but
the Temple, which was designed and executed by a
man miraculously endowed for the purpose. A high
antiquarian authority tells us that "pure Shemites
had no art."[1] The lack of architectural and artistic
skill is no mark of the absence of the higher elements
of character.[2] 3rdly, With regard to the necessity of
the slave trade, we remark, without attempting to

[1] Rev. Stuart Poole, of the British Museum, before the British
Association, 1864.

[2] Rev. Dr. Goulburn, in his reply to Dr. Temple's celebrated
Essay on the "Education of the World," has the following suggestive remark : "We commend to Dr. Temple's notice the pregnant
fact, that in the earliest extant history of mankind it is stated that
arts, both ornamental and useful, (and arts are the great medium of
civilization,) took their rise in the family of Cain. In the line of
Seth we find none of this mental and social development."—*Replies
to Essays and Reviews*, p. 34. When the various causes now co-op-
erating shall have produced a higher religious sense among the nations, and a corresponding revolution shall have taken place in the
estimation now put upon material objects, the effort may be to show,
to his disparagement—if we could imagine such an unamiable undertaking as compatible with the high state of progress then attained—
that the Negro was at the foundation of all material development.

enter into the secret counsels of the Most High, that
without the foreign slave trade Africa would have
been a great deal more accessible to civilization, and
would now, had peaceful and legitimate intercourse
been kept up with her from the middle of the fifteenth
century, be taking her stand next to Europe in civilization, science, and religion. When, four hundred
years ago, the Portuguese discovered this coast, they
found the natives living in considerable peace and
quietness, and with a certain degree of prosperity.
Internal feuds, of course, the tribes sometimes had,
but by no means so serious as they afterward became
under the stimulating influence of the slave trade.
From all we can gather, the tribes in this part of
Africa lived in a condition not very different from that
of the greater portion of Europe in the Middle Ages.
There was the same oppression of the weak by the
strong; the same resistance by the weak, often taking
the form of general rebellion; the same private and
hereditary wars; the same strongholds in every
prominent position; the same dependence of the people upon the chief who happened to be in power; the
same contentedness of the masses with the tyrannical
rule. But there was industry and activity, and in
every town there were manufactures, and they sent
across the continent to Egypt and the Barbary States
other articles besides slaves.

✓ The permanence for centuries of the social and
political states of the Africans at home must be
attributed, first, to the isolation of the people from the
progressive portion of mankind; and, secondly, to the
blighting influence of the traffic introduced among

them by Europeans. Had not the demand arisen in America for African laborers, and had European nations inaugurated regular traffic with the coast, the natives would have shown themselves as impressible for change, as susceptible of improvement, as capable of acquiring knowledge and accumulating wealth, as the natives of Europe. Combination of capital and co-operation of energies would have done for this land what they have done for others. Private enterprise, (which has been entirely destroyed by the nefarious traffic,) encouraged by humane intercourse with foreign lands, would have developed agriculture, manufactures, and commerce; would have cleared, drained, and fertilized the country, and built towns; would have improved the looms, brought in plows, steam-engines, printing-presses, machines, and the thousand processes and appliances by which the comfort, progress, and usefulness of mankind are secured. But, alas! *Dis aliter visum.*

> "Freighted with curses was the bark that bore
> The spoilers of the West to Guinea's shore;
> Heavy with groans of anguish blew the gales
> That swelled that fatal bark's returning sails:
> Loud and perpetual o'er the Atlantic's waves,
> For guilty ages, rolled the tide of slaves;
> A tide that knew no fall, no turn, no rest—
> Constant as day and night from East to West,
> Still widening, deepening, swelling in its course
> With boundless ruin and resistless force."—Montgomery.

But although, amid the violent shocks of those changes and disasters to which the natives of this outraged land have been subject, their knowledge of the elegant arts, brought from the East, declined, they never entirely lost the *necessary* arts of life. They still understand the workmanship of iron, and, in some sections of the country, of gold. The loom and the forge are in constant use among them. In remote regions, where they have no intercourse with Europeans, they raise large herds of cattle and innumerable sheep and goats; capture and train horses, build well-laid-out towns, cultivate extensive fields, and manufacture earthenware and woolen and cotton cloths. Commander Foote says: "The Negro arts are respectable, and would have been more so had not disturbance and waste come with the slave-trade." [1]

And in our own times, on the West Coast of Africa, a native development of literature has been brought to light of genuine home-growth. The Vey people, residing half way between Sierra Leone and Cape Mesurado, have within the last thirty years invented a syllabic alphabet, with which they are now writing their own language, and by which they are maintaining among themselves an extensive epistolary correspondence. In 1849 the Church Missionary Society in London, having heard of this invention, authorized their missionary, Rev. S. W. Koelle, to investigate the subject. Mr. Koelle travelled into the interior, and brought away three manuscripts, with translations. The symbols are phonetic, and constitute a syllabarium, not an alphabet; they are nearly two hundred in number. They have been learned so generally that Vey boys in Monrovia frequently receive communications from their friends in the Vey country, to which they readily respond. The Church Missionary Society

[1] "Africa and the American Flag," p. 52.

have had a font of type cast in this new character, and several little tracts have been printed and circulated among the tribe. The principal inventor of this alphabet is now dead; but it is supposed that he died in the Christian faith, having acquired some knowledge of the way of salvation through the medium of this character of his own invention.[1] Dr. Wilson says:

This invention is one of the most remarkable achievements of this or any other age, and is itself enough to silence forever the cavils and sneers of those who think so contemptuously of the intellectual endowments of the African race.

Though "the idea of communicating thoughts in writing was probably suggested by the use of Arabic among the Mandingoes," yet the invention was properly original, showing the existence of genius in the native African who has never been in foreign slavery, and proves that he carries in his bosom germs of intellectual development and self-elevation, which would have enabled him to advance regularly in the path of progress, had it not been for the blighting influence of the slave-trade.

Now are we to believe that such a people have been doomed, by the terms of any curse, to be the "servant of servants," as some upholders of Negro slavery have taught? Would it not have been a very singular theory that a people destined to servitude should begin, the very first thing, as we have endeavored to show, to found "great cities," organize kingdoms, and establish rule—putting up structures

[1] Wilson's "Western Africa," p. 95, and "Princeton Review for July, 1858," p. 488.

which have come down to this day as a witness to their *superiority* over all their contemporaries—and that, by a Providential decree, the people whom they had been fated to serve should be held in bondage by them four hundred years?

The remarkable enterprise of the Cushite hero, Nimrod ; his establishment of imperial power, as an advance on patriarchal government ; the strength of the Egypt of Mizraim, and its long domination over the house of Israel ; and the evidence which now and then appears, that even Phut (who is the obscurest in his fortunes of all the Hamite race) maintained a relation to the descendants of Shem which was far from servile or subject ; do all clearly tend to limit the application of Noah's maledictory prophecy to the precise terms in which it was indited : "Cursed be Canaan ; a servant of servants shall he " (not Cush, not Mizraim, not Phut, but he) " be to his brethren." If we then confine the imprecation to Canaan, we can without difficulty trace its accomplishment in the subjugation of the tribes which issued from him to the children of Israel from the time of Joshua to that of David. Here would be verified Canaan's servile relation to Shem ; and when imperial Rome finally wrested the sceptre from Judah, and, "dwelling in the tents of Shem," occupied the East and whatever remnants of Canaan were left in it, would not this accomplish that further prediction that Japheth, too, should be lord of Canaan, and that (as it would seem to be tacitly implied) mediately, through his occupancy of the tents of Shem ? [1]

A vigorous writer in the "Princeton Review" has the following :

The Ethiopian race, from whom the modern Negro or African stock are undoubtedly descended, can claim as early a history, with the exception of the Jews,[2] as any living people

[1] Dr. Peter Holmes, Oxford, England.

[2] The Jews not excepted. Where were they when the Pyramids were built?

on the face of the earth.   History, as well as the monumental discoveries, gives them a place in ancient history as far back as Egypt herself, if not farther.   But what has become of the contemporaneous nations of antiquity, as well as others of much later origin ?   Where are the Numidians, Mauritanians, and other powerful names, who once held sway over all Northern Africa ?   They have been swept away from the earth, or dwindled down to a handful of modern Copts and Berbers of doubtful descent.

The Ethiopian, or African race, on the other hand, though they have long since lost all the civilization which once existed on the Upper Nile, have, nevertheless, continued to increase and multiply, until they are now, with the exception of the Chinese, the largest single family of men on the face of the earth. They have extended themselves in every direction over that great continent, from the southern borders of the Great Sahara to the Cape of Good Hope, and from the Atlantic to the Indian Ocean, and are thus constituted masters of at least three-fourths of the habitable portions of this great continent. And this progress has been made, be it remembered, in despite of the prevalence of the foreign slave-trade, which has carried off so many of their people ; of the ceaseless internal feuds and wars that have been waged among themselves ; and of a conspiracy, as it were, among all surrounding nations, to trample out their national existence.   Surely their history is a remarkable one ; but not more so, perhaps, than is foreshadowed in the prophecies of the Old Scriptures.   God has watched over and preserved these people through all the vicissitudes of their unwritten history, and no doubt for some great purpose of mercy toward them, as well as for the display of the glory of his own grace and providence ; and we may expect to have a full revelation of this purpose and glory as soon as the everlasting Gospel is made known to these benighted millions. [1]

One palpable reason may be assigned why the Ethiopian race has continued to exist under the most

[1] "Princeton Review," July 1858, pp. 448, 449.

adverse circumstances, while other races and tribes have perished from the earth ; it is this : *they have never been a bloodthirsty or avaricious people.* From the beginning of their history to the present time their work has been constructive, except when they have been stimulated to wasting wars by the covetous foreigner. They have *built up* in Asia, Africa, and America. They have not delighted in despoiling and oppressing others. The nations enumerated by the reviewer just quoted, and others besides them—all warlike and fighting nations—have passed away or dwindled into utter insignificance. They seem to have been consumed by their own fierce internal passions. The Ethiopians, though brave and powerful, were not a fighting people, that is, were not fond of fighting for the sake of humbling and impoverishing other people. Every reader of history will remember the straightforward, brave, and truly Christian answer returned by the King of the Ethiopians to Cambyses, who was contemplating an invasion of Ethiopia, as recorded by Herodotus. For the sake of those who may not have access to that work, we reproduce the narrative here. About five hundred years before Christ, Cambyses, the great Persian warrior, while invading Egypt, planned an expedition against the Ethiopians ; but before proceeding upon the belligerent enterprises he sent

"Spies, in the first instance, who were to see the table of the sun, which was said to exist among the Ethiopians, and besides, to explore other things, and, to cover their design, they were to carry presents to the King. . . . When the messengers of Cambyses arrived among the Ethiopians they gave the presents to the King, and addressed him as follows : "Cambyses, King of the Persians, desirous of becoming your friend and ally, has sent us, bidding us confer with you, and he presents you with these gifts, which are such as he himself most delights in."

But the Ethiopian knowing that they came as spies, spoke thus to them :

"Neither has the King of Persia sent you with these presents to me because he valued my alliance, nor do you speak the truth, for you are come as spies of my kingdom. Nor is he a just man ; for if he were just he would not desire any other territory than his own ; nor would he reduce people into servitude who have done him no injury. However, give him this bow, and say these words to him : 'The King of the Ethiopians advises the King of the Persians, when the Persians can thus easily draw a bow of this size, then to make war on the Macrobian Ethiopians with more numerous forces ; but until that time let him thank the gods, who have not inspired the sons of the Ethiopians with the desire of adding another land to their own.' " [1]

Are these a people, with such remarkable antecedents, and in the whole of whose history the hand of God is so plainly seen, to be treated with the contempt which they usually suffer in the lands of their bondage? When we notice the scornful indifference with which the Negro is spoken of by certain politicians in America, we fancy that the attitude of Pharaoh and the aristocratic Egyptians must have been precisely similar toward the Jews. We fancy we see one of the magicians in council, after the first visit of Moses demanding the release of the Israelites, rising up with indignation and pouring out a torrent

[1] Herodotus, iii. 17–22.

of scornful invective such as any rabid anti-Negro
politician might now indulge in.

What privileges are those that these degraded
Hebrews are craving? What are they? Are they
not slaves and the descendants of slaves? What have
they or their ancestors ever done? What *can* they
do? They did not come hither of their own accord.
The first of them was brought to this country a slave,
sold to us by his own brethren. Others followed him,
refugees from the famine of an impoverished country.
What do they know about managing liberty or controlling themselves? They are idle; they are idle.
Divert their attention from their idle dreams by additional labor and more exacting tasks.

But what have the ancestors of Negroes ever done?
Let Professor Rawlinson answer, as a summing up of
our discussion. Says the learned Professor :

For the last three thousand years the world has been mainly
indebted for its advancement to the Semitic and Indo-Euro-
pean races ; *but it was otherwise in the first ages.* Egypt and
Babylon, Mizraim and Nimrod—both descendants of Ham—led
the way, and acted as the pioneers of mankind in the various
untrodden fields of art, literature, and science. Alphabetic
writing, astronomy, history, chronology, architecture, plastic
art, sculpture, navigation, agriculture, textile industry, seem
all of them to have had their origin in one or other of these two
countries. The beginnings may have been often humble
enough. We may laugh at the rude picture-writing, the un-
couth brick pyramid, the coarse fabric, the homely and ill-
shapen instruments, as they present themselves to our notice
in the remains of these ancient nations ; but they are really
worthier of our admiration than of our ridicule. The inven-
tors of any art are among the greatest benefactors of their race,

and mankind at the present day lies under infinite obligations
to the genius of these early ages.[1]

There are now, probably, few thoughtful and cultivated men in the United States who are prepared to
advocate the application of the curse of Noah to all
the descendants of Ham. The experience of the last
eight years must have convinced the most ardent
theorizer on the subject. Facts have not borne out
their theory and predictions concerning the race. The
Lord by his outstretched arm has dashed their syllo-
gisms to atoms, scattered their dogmas to the winds,
detected the partiality and exaggerating tendency of
their method, and shown the injustice of that heartless
philosophy and that unrelenting theology which con-
signed a whole race of men to hopeless and intermi-
nable servitude.

It is difficult, nevertheless, to understand how, with
the history of the past accessible, the facts of the
present before their eyes, and the prospect of a
clouded future, or unvailed only to disclose the indefinite numerical increase of Europeans in the land, the
blacks of the United States can hope for any distinct,
appreciable influence in the country. We cannot
perceive on what grounds the most sanguine among
their friends can suppose that there will be so decisive
a revolution of popular feeling in favor of their *proteges*
as to make them at once the political and social equals
of their former masters. Legislation cannot secure
them this equality in the United States any more
than it has secured it for the blacks in the West
Indies. During the time of slavery everything in the

---

[1] "Five Great Monarchies," vol. i. pp. 75, 76.

laws, in the customs, in the education of the people
was contrived with the single view of degrading the
Negro in his own estimation and that of others. Now
is it possible to change in a day the habits and
character which centuries of oppression have entailed?
We think not. More than one generation, it appears
to us, must pass away before the full effect of education, enlightenment, and social improvement will be
visible among the blacks. Meanwhile they are being
gradually absorbed by the Caucasian; and before
their social equality comes to be conceded they will
have lost their identity altogether; a result, in our
opinion, extremely undesirable, as we believe that,
as Negroes, they might accomplish a great work
which others cannot perform. But even if they
should not pass away in the mighty embrace of their
numerous white neighbors; grant that they could continue to live in the land, a distinct people, with the
marked peculiarities they possess, having the same
color and hair, badges of a former thraldom—is it to
be supposed that they can ever overtake a people who
so largely outnumber them, and a large proportion of
whom are endowed with wealth, leisure, and the habits
and means of study and self-improvement? If they improve in culture and training, as in time they no
doubt will, and become intelligent and educated, there
may rise up individuals among them, here and there,
who will be respected and honored by the whites;
but it is plain that, as a class, their inferiority will
never cease until they cease to be a distinct people,
possessing peculiarities which suggest antecedents of
servility and degradation.

2*

We pen these lines with the most solemn feelings
—grieved that so many strong, intelligent, and energetic black men should be wasting time and labor in
a fruitless contest, which, expended in the primitive
land of their fathers—a land that so much needs them
—would produce in a comparatively short time results
of incalculable importance. But what can we do?
Occupying this distant stand-point—an area of Negro
freedom and a scene for untrammeled growth and
development, but a wide and ever-expanding field for
benevolent effort ; an outlying or surrounding wilderness to be reclaimed ; barbarism of ages to be brought
over to Christian life—we can only repeat with un-
diminished earnestness the wish we have frequently
expressed elsewhere, that the *eyes of the blacks may be
opened to discern their true mission and destiny ;* that,
making their escape from the house of bondage, they
may *betake themselves to their ancestral home, and assist
in constructing a Christian* AFRICAN EMPIRE. For we
believe that as descendants of Ham had a share, as
the most prominent actors on the scene, in the founding of cities and in the organization of government, so
members of the same family, developed under different
circumstances, will have an important part in the
closing of the great drama.

" Time's noblest offspring is the last."

II.

THE KORAN. AFRICAN MOHAMMEDANISM,

BY TAYLER LEWIS, LL.D.

From the New York Independent, April 6, 1871.

SEVERAL months ago Dr. Pinney, the well-known agent of the Colonization Society, brought to me a manuscript copy of the Koran, written by a Mandingo Negro. It commenced abruptly with the XIXth *Surat,* or chapter, but from thence continued unbroken to the end.

It was very beautifully written in the large, bold hand that distinguishes the Western style of Arabic writing, and bore quite a strong resemblance to some of the older and more distinct specimens of Arabic chirography given in De Sacy's Grammar. It had interlined, or rather between each verse, and sometimes between clauses and single words, a running commentary in red ink, and occupying about as much space as the text. This was made up by brief extracts from the great Koranic commentators, such as Beidhawi and Zamakhshari. A peculiar feature, however, was the continual recurrence of very plain grammatical notes, given in the peculiar technics of Arabic grammar, but evidently adapted to young and uninstructed minds. They pointed out sometimes the number of

the noun or the object of the verb, and very frequently
the meaning of the more learned or less known words.
The inference from this was that it had been tran-
scribed from some copy much used in schools.   Dr.
Pinney thought it had been written from memory.
This would seem hardly possible; and yet the wonder
is much diminished by what we are told of Mohammedan teachers, some of whom have read and recited
the Koran hundreds and even thousands of times.
There could be no doubt, however, of its having been
written in Liberia, in a very rapid manner, and by one
removed from aids he might have had in his native
home.   The very appearance of this curious volume
gave evidence of the way in which it had been made
up; for it was nothing more, externally, than a coarse
folio ledger, like those employed in the custom-house,
and furnished to the native scribe for this particular
service.

I could not help feeling a wonderful interest in this
strange book. It seemed like a stream of light coming
from one of the darkest places of the earth, as many,
in their ignorance, have regarded it.   This single
volume, thus constructed, brought evidence of many
other things along with it. · It told us of religion
where we had thought there existed only the grossest
forms of Fetish idolatry, for the most orthodox
Christian need not hesitate to say that Mohammedanism is religion, pure religion, as far as it goes. The
Koran is a very devout book. There appears everywhere in it the *Yirath Jehowah*, or religion in its pure
primary etymological idea, as "the fear of the Lord
is the beginning of wisdom." Besides its pure mono-

theistic aspect, Mohammedanism is eminently a religion of prayer, though lacking the Christian idea of a divine human mediatorship. God as lawgiver, as judge, as an ever-watchful Providence, never losing sight of individuals or nations, appears on almost every page of the Koran. It represents him as the executor of a stern retribution, and yet as exhibiting a melting tenderness that reminds us of the strong contrasts of the Hebrew prophets. In short, there are to be found in it, most powerfully expressed, those fearful aspects of religion which give to the more loving attributes of Deity their most precious value, but which seem to be losing their dread conservative force, even in what we call our "evangelical theology." The Resurrection, the great and final judgment, the doom of the wicked—it would be difficult to find language stronger than that in which the Koran sets forth these, whilst ever holding up the thought of a particular Providence, and of a retribution that never slumbers, even in this world. A thing, however, to be especially noted is the strong contrast it seems fond of presenting between the present and the future life; although its pictures of the latter may be justly blamed as having too much of a sensual aspect. This contrast appears in the very names so oft occurring. The present world is *dunya*, the *near*, the *mean*, the *inferior*; it is *ajelun*, the *hastening, transient*, swiftly *passing away;* the life to come (the *acherat*, or after state) is *chuldun*, the *abiding*, the *perennial*, the *eternal*.

We may, as Christians, fearlessly admit those excellencies of the Koran, when we call to mind an important and even essential distinction between it

and other books called sacred, which some are fond of
placing in parallelism with the Christian Scriptures.
The Koran is a reflection of the Bible ; it is grounded
on the old Testament Scriptures ; it would never have
been had not Judaism and Christianity been before it.
It professes to be a revival of the grand old patriarchal or Abrahamic worship. It might almost be
called an apocryphal book of the Bible, ranking
among writings which we esteem most valuable or
even sacred, and having a reflection, as it were, of the
Bible inspiration, though we cannot regard them as
canonical, or possessed of the same Christ-sanctioned
authority. The Koran admits the divine authority of
the Scriptures, both New and Old. It speaks not
only reverently, but tenderly and lovingly, of Jesus,
or " *Isa ben Maryam*, the " Word of Truth," as it calls
him, *Surat* xix. 35 ; and it is only in some few places
of the later chapters that there is anything incon-
sistent with this spirit. Throughout the better part
of the book the *Kafirs* who are to be forced into truth
by the sword are the unclean and bloody Pagan
idolaters.

Belief in Mohammedanism furnishes a more en-
couraging basis for missionary effort than can be
found among the followers of the worn-out religions of
Brahma, Buddha, and Confucius. The very fact that
the Koranic religion is sharply controversial is an
evidence of its vitality. It has something to contend
for, and we ought to esteem it the more highly on that
very account. It is better to meet the zealous Islamite
in this way than to encounter the meaningless panthe-
ism of the Hindu, who has lately been so much

applauded by his fellow Nothingarians in England, or
the stolid indifference of the Chinese, who says:
" Our Josh, your Josh ; your Josh for you, our Josh
for us ; all very good Josh." A contest with a religion that has such a living basis to it, however
erroneous or deficient we may esteem it, is all the
more hopeful in the end; and, for his own soul's
health, the missionary might well prefer these Koran-
taught Mandingo Negroes, as his field of labor, to the
conscience-deadened inhabitants of Thibet, China, or
Japan.

The contrast between the religions is not greater
than that between the books by which they are
represented. · Take the cold abstractions, the dry
mysticism, the thin philosophisms, which are held up
to our admiration from the Hindoo books, whatever
may be their date, or the poor, barren worldliness
which is all that we get from the best selections made
from the writings of Confucius ; compare them with
the glowing devotion, the sublime earnestness, the
pure, distinct, and lofty theism of the Koran, and we
cease to wonder at the fact of its triumph wherever it
met those lifeless creeds. It was not from age alone
that they were powerless ; but because they never had
in them that strong *conservative* element which distinguishes the Christian, Jewish, and Mohammedan
theism ; in other words, "*the fear of the Lord*," the
awe of a holy, personal, retributive, sin-hating, right-
loving God. We thus understand, too, why it is that
Mohammedanism has so much vigor at the present
day.

The Koran is, indeed, a wonderful book. As a

short yet convincing proof of this, I would refer the
reader to an admirable article by Prof. Blyden, of
Liberia College, in the January number of the *Methodist Quarterly Review*.[1] It gives a remarkably clear
and striking account of African Mohammedanism.
Taken in connection with another article on the same
subject, and for the same *Quarterly*, written a number
of years ago, by Prof. Dwight, of Brooklyn, it de-
serves the thorough and respectful study of all
Christian scholars.[1] They would make us ashamed,
as we ought to be, of that vile prejudice against the
Negro which still possesses the minds of so many,
even among those who claim to be his friend. A
special value, however, of this well-written article of
Prof. Blyden (himself a colored man[2]) is the intelligent and scholarly testimony it bears to the literary
excellence of the Koran. This he defends, not only
against the common ignorant estimate, but in opposition to the great authority of Gibbon, who pronounces
the book a series of "incoherent rhapsodies." Boldly,
yet most justly and intelligently does Prof. Blyden
maintain that the great historian ventures an opinion
upon a matter of which, from his ignorance of the
Arabic, as well as from his own peculiar irreligious
idiosyncrasy, he was a very incompetent judge. He
misunderstood the poetical character of the Koran,

[1] Both of which are inserted in this volume.

[2] I am almost ashamed to say this, even in a parenthesis. It has
too much the look of a sort of patronizing condescension, or of
making a wonder of what should be no wonder at all. There is no
such thing as color in the literary world. There are, however, certain readers for whose information it was thought best to let it
stand.

and was unable to estimate the great loss it suffered by being stripped of its very musical and remarkable rhythm. This is well shown by the author of the article. But the argument may be carried still further. Not only does the thought, in such case, lose the added charm of its musical accompaniment; but is, in itself, essentially injured. It is not merely the loss of euphony. By regarding it as prose, the reader is placed in a wrong position for judging of its ideal merit. The poetical portion of the Bible suffers in this way; but less, because the rhythm, consisting mainly in the parallelism, which is still, in a measure, preserved in the poorest translation, keeps up some feeling that it is poetry we are reading. In a translation, the Koran appears as the baldest prose. It suffers without any compensation; and the reason can be briefly stated. The strength as well as the beauty of poetry consists in the clear feeling of its emotional transitions. There is a real train of thought; and it is all the more striking, when we perceive it, because its links are in the feeling, rather than in the logical understanding. A figure in one verse suggests an idea in that which follows. The flow of emotion carries us over the interval. We are on the lookout for transitions of this kind; when they come, we are prepared for them. There is something of a pleasant surprise, indeed; but this adds vigor to the emotion, and clearness to the thought of which the emotion is the life. We learn to recognize such connections, slight as they may appear in themselves, with even a livelier appreciation than those of a closer kind. This is because we are reading it as poetry, and are kept

in this channel of feeling by the constant suggestion
of the rhythm. Now, when read as prose, not only is
the rhythm lost, on which the thought runs smoothly
(or *on its wheels*, as Solomon says, Prov. xxv. 11), but
the mind is turned altogether in a wrong direction for
apprehending rightly the train of ideas. We immediately expect the closer logical connections. Missing
these, and not finding the emotional links that supply
their place, we pronounce it, as Gibbon did, an un-
meaning, incoherent rhapsody.

Another Mandingo Arabic manuscript, in the same
style with that of the Koran first mentioned, has been
printed from photographic plates, through the liberality of H. M. Schieffelin, of New York, and generously
sent to persons interested in such studies. It is a letter from the King of Musadu, a town far in the interior, to the President of Liberia, and written by the Negro schoolmaster of the place. It possesses a similar
interest in respect to its chirography, the religious feeling it occasionally exhibits, and its Koranic references.
Its frequent blessings and invocations may be as serious, or they may be as formal, as the reciprocal salutations of Boaz and his reapers—Ruth ii. 4; but they
indicate what may be called the communal religious
interest—stereotyped, it may be, into formalism, yet
showing an original source once warm with religious
zeal, and still preserving a measure of at least social
vitality. Another interest of this letter is in the
glimpse it gives us of Mandingo literature, as shown
by its citations from the *Makamat*, or seances, of Hariri, the most renowned, perhaps, among the choice
Arabian classics, and of which De Sacy has given

such a splendid edition. There is a temptation to go into a fuller account of the Mandingo culture, as thus exhibited, but this communication is already too long, and sufficient has been said, perhaps, to arouse the attention of those who may have interest in such out-of-the-way matters.

III.

CONDITION AND CHARACTER OF NEGROES IN AFRICA.

BY THEODORE DWIGHT, ESQ.

From the Methodist Quarterly Review, January, 1869.

THE erroneous impressions which prevail in the civilized world respecting the condition of the Negro race in Africa are discreditable to the intelligence of the age. The people of the United States are doubly blamable for their false views on this subject, because we owe debts to that portion of our fellow-men for ages of wrongs inflicted on them for our benefit, and because, with ample means within our reach for correcting our erroneous opinions, we generally neglect them, and still persist in denying to Negroes those intellectual faculties and moral qualities which the Creator has bestowed on the entire human family. With the books of recent travellers in Africa in their hands, it may well be wondered at that even our most

intelligent and humane writers have not yet appealed
to the testimony of Bowen, Livingstone, and Barth, to
prove that millions of pagan Negroes, in different parts
of that continent, have been for ages in the practice
of some of the most important arts of life, dwelling in
comfort and generally at peace; while many other
millions have been raised to a considerable degree of
civilization by Mohammedism, and long existed in
powerful independent states; under various changes,
it is true, but perhaps not so many or great as those
through which the principal nations of "civilized
Europe" passed during the same periods.

To refer to but one portion of the vast regions of
Africa inhabited by the Black Race, namely, that extending along the southern border of the Great
Desert, we find there, between the tenth and twentieth
degrees of north latitude, five or six kingdoms, most
of which have been in existence several centuries, and
some a thousand years, mostly under the influence of
Mohammedan institutions. These are everywhere
similar, so far as they prevail, establishing fixed laws,
customs, arts, and learning; and, although abounding
in errors and evils on the one side, embracing benefits
on the other which are not enjoyed by such portions
of the Negro race as remain in paganism. The Koran,
as is well known, has copied from the Hebrew Scriptures many of the attributes of God and the doctrines
of morality, with certain just views of the nature,
capacities, duties, and destiny of man; and these are
so faithfully taught, that they are conspicuous in the
writings of many of the numerous authors in Mohammedan countries, and often displayed, in a more or

less satisfactory degree, in the characters and lives of those educated in them.

Want of space in these pages must necessarily limit our remarks to very narrow bounds, and we shall therefore be unable to present many details which would interest the reader, and can give only a few facts relating to Mohammedan learning, its nature, institutions, and results. This forms an essential part of the Moslem system, and has long been in operation on large families of the Negro race, and moulded them after the civilized model of the Arabs and Moors. ~~Unlike Popery~~, it favors, nay, requires, as a fundamental principle, the free and universal reading and study of their sacred book; and, instead of withholding it from the people under penalties of death and perdition, it establishes schools for all classes, primarily to teach its languages and doctrines. Extracts from the Koran form the earliest reading lessons of children, and the commentaries and other works founded upon it furnish the principal subjects of the advanced studies.

As this has always been the practice, it may not seem strange that learning flourished among the Moors, in Spain, during the Dark Ages of Europe, ~~while Popery so long overshadowed the nations with her worse than Egyptian darkness.~~ Readers who have neglected Africa may not be prepared to believe that schools of different grades have existed for centuries in various interior negro countries, and under the provisions of law, in which even the poor are educated at the public expense, and in which the deserving are carried on many years through long courses of regular instruction. Nor is this system always confined to the Arabic language, or to the works of Arabian writers. A number of native languages have been reduced to writing, books have been translated from the Arabic, and original works have been written in them. Schools also have been kept in which native languages are taught. Indeed, one of the most gratifying evidences has thus been furnished of the favorable influences exerted by the unrestricted use, as well as the general diffusion of the knowledge of letters; while the truth is not less certain, because hitherto unknown, that large portions of the African Continent lie open to the access of Christian influences through channels thus prepared by education.

These and other facts, which we shall not stop to mention, make it appear wonderful indeed that the African race should be judged by us only from that small and unfortunate portion of it found in the western continent. Where is the excuse for looking only at ten millions, more or less, of slaves and descendants of slaves in America, and entirely neglecting to inquire into the condition and character, the history and capacities of the hundred or more millions of negroes in their native country, who have had some opportunity to show what they are capable of? It is now time for public attention in the United States to be directed to Africa, and an attentive perusal of the most recent travels will afford the reader the details of many things which we can only cursorily mention in this article, while earlier publications will be found to afford confirmation of some of the most important facts. It certainly will bring more compunction to the

hearts of the humane among us, to learn that the
race which we have been accustomed to despise, as
well as to ill treat, still lie under a load of evils per-
petuated by the prejudices prevailing even among
many of the most enlightened Christians; and it will
be surprising to be told, that among the victims of
the slave-trade among us have been men of learning
and pure and exalted characters, who have been
treated-like beasts of the field by those who claimed
a purer religion.

About a hundred years ago a report reached England that a young African slave in Maryland, named
Job-ben-Solomon, was able to write Arabic, and
appeared to be well-educated and well-bred. Measures were taken to secure his release, and he was sent
to England, where he assisted Sir Hans Sloane in
translating Arabic, and acquired a character of the
highest kind for intelligence, judgment, morality, and
kindness of heart. He was sent up the Gambia River
to Bundu, where he was received with the warmest
welcome, and the truth of his story was fully proved,
he being the son of the hereditary prince of that part
of the country. Several other Africans have been
known at different periods, in different parts of America, somewhat resembling Job-ben-Solomon in acquirements; but, unfortunately, no full account of
any of them has ever been published. The writer has
made many efforts to remedy this defect, and has
obtained some information from a few individuals.
But there are insuperable difficulties in the way in
slave countries, arising from the jealousies of masters,
and other causes, which quite discouraged a gentle-

man who made exertions in the South some years
since, and compelled him to abandon the undertaking
in despair, although he had resided in Africa, and had
both the taste and the ability necessary to success.
The writer has found a few native Africans in the
North, of whom only three were able to write, and
only one had opportunity to give him long personal
interviews. "Prince," or "Abder-rahman," he saw
once in New-York, about the year 1830; from "Morro," or "Omar-ben-Sayeed," long living in Fayetteville, N. C., he procured a sketch of his life in Arabic;
and from "Old Paul," or "Lahmen Kibby," he obtained a great amount of most interesting information.
That venerable old man was liberated in 1835, after,
being about forty years a slave in South Carolina,
Alabama, and other southern states, and spent about
a year in New York, under the care of the Colonization Society, while waiting for a vessel to take him
back to his native country. The writer held numerous and prolonged interviews with him, and found
him deeply interested in making his communications
concerning his native country and people, as well as
his own history, for the purpose of having them
published, for the information of Americans. He
often said, "There are good men in America, but all
are very ignorant of Africa. Write down what I tell
you exactly as I say it, and be careful to distinguish
between what I have seen and what I have only
heard other people speak of. They may have made
some mistakes; but if you put down exactly what I
say, by and by, when good men go to Africa, they will
say, *Paul told the truth.*"

The writer has since arranged and written out the voluminous notes which he took from the lips of the old man, (some of them in stenography,) and has added many extracts from travellers and others, all confirmatory of his statements, but has never found an opportunity to publish them. It appears that his aged informant was in possession of many facts still unknown even to the most learned of America and Europe, which the most bold and enterprising travellers have failed to discover, though risking life, and even losing it, in the attempt. Three or four pages on the subject, published in 1836 in the proceedings of the American Lyceum, attracted attention in Europe, and led the Paris Geographical Society to make repeated applications for more information; and Dr. Latham quoted them as one of the only three authorities on the Sereculy language, in his learned paper presented to the British Scientific Association. Dr. Coëlle, missionary of the Church Missionary Society, has since given a brief vocabulary of that language, (Paul's native tongue,) but without any particular information of the people. They are one of the negro families before alluded to, which are intermingled, without being amalgamated, over extensive regions in Nigritia, partly Mohammedan and partly Pagan.

His native country is Footah, peopled by several races, all governed by the Foolahs. This is the most western of the seven or eight separate and independent states or kingdoms lying in a remarkably regular series, and in a straight line along the southern boundary of the Great Desert, or Zahara, from Sene-

3

gambia to Nubia and Abyssinia. These have been recently visited by that learned and energetic traveller, Dr. Barth, whose three octavo volumes contain a vast amount of information concerning those fertile and populous regions, their history and condition, so materially affected by the influence of Mohammedism, which has prevailed in some of them for a thousand years. Why is it that ignorance of those countries still prevails among us? Why is the kingdom of Footah still so unknown, though only about three hundred miles distant from the Atlantic coast, and since the English and French have had trading posts on the Gambia and the Senegal for two hundred years? Because, as the Rev. Mr. Poole mentions in a late work, foreigners are still afraid to leave the rivers' side, having a dread of the wild beasts and savage men who are supposed to threaten death to every intruder who may venture to pass through the forests and swamps, which were long ravaged by slave-hunters, who sent their human victims to America. The Gambia and Senegal rise in the high grounds in the southern parts of Footah, and flow through much of its territory northward, and then turn west, to make their way through the low and hot district just mentioned to the coast. Only their lower waters are navigable, and only Park, Caillée, the Landers, and a few other travellers, have ever gone beyond the heads of navigation when in search of Timbuctoo or the Niger; and the Rev. William Fox, the English Wesleyan missionary, who endeavored to establish a mission in Bundu about eighteen years ago. None of all these ever saw anything of Footah

except the extreme northern portion; and all were
ignorant of the numerous languages and dialects of
the various tribes through which they passed. Neither has any white man ever crossed the boundary of
that first of the Mohammedan negro states, from
Sierra Leone or Liberia, which lie below the Gambia. Mr. Seymour, a mulatto man of education and
enterprise, originally from Hartford, went on foot
from Monrovia, about four years ago, to near the
southern confines of Footah, and found a varied, rich,
and populous country, with numerous towns and
villages, immense fields of rice, cotton, corn, vegetables, etc.; the people industrious and hospitable,
manufacturing their clothes and iron, with regular
fairs for the purchase and sale of numerous articles
of domestic and foreign production. As one evidence
of the erroneous impressions common in the world
respecting the habits of Africans, it may be mentioned that in that region, as in Yoruba, (a country
fifteen hundred or two thousand miles distant from
it,) the women not only sweep their houses frequently,
but carry the dust outside of the gates of the towns.

"Old Paul" was born in the southern part of
Footah, and in his early childhood used to bring
water in a calabash to his mother from the Cabab,
one of the head streams of the Jalibah. He after-
wards lived in the cities of Kebbe, or Kibby, and
Bundu, where he spent many years in studying under
different masters. On several occasions he accompanied caravans and armies on mercantile and military expeditions into adjacent and more distant
countries, and his accounts of these abound in details

of great novelty and interest. The same may be said
of his communications on the history, customs, arts,
religions, learning, languages, books, schools, teachers, travellers, productions, trade, etc., of the mixed
people among whom he lived. In respect to its
varied population, his country resembles the unex-
plored regions before mentioned, lying between it and
the sea-coast; but as Footah is a Mohammedan country, the religion of the false prophet affords a bond
of union strong enough to hold the heterogeneous
multitude under one government, and generally in the
peaceful enjoyment of the laws, arts, and learning
which belong to a Mohammedan community, being
provided for by the Koran and claimed by its believers. When we bear in mind that the chief attributes of God and some of the principles of morality
were copied into that book from the Hebrew Scriptures, we may realize something of the difference
between Mohammedan and Pagan countries in Africa.
One great advantage of the former consists in the use
of letters. Arabic is taught in schools wherever the
priests can find pupils; and such is their proselyting
spirit, or rather (as we may truly say of many of them)
their humane desire to diffuse the faith in which they
conscientiously believe, that they are sometimes seen
in Liberia, Sierra Leone, and other places far from
their homes, teaching children to write the Arabic
characters on the sand.

Paul was a schoolmaster in Footah, after pursuing
a long course of preparatory studies, and said that he
had an aunt who was much more learned than himself, and eminent for her superior acquirements and

for her skill in teaching. Schools, he said, were generally established through the country, provision being made by law for educating children of all classes, the poor being taught gratuitously. All the details of the system he was ready to give in answer to inquiries, including the methods, rules, books, etc. The books, of course, were all in manuscript; and what has seemed difficult of belief, even by well-informed persons in our country, several native African languages were written in Arabic characters. He gave a catalogue of about thirty books in his own mother tongue, (the Sereculy or Serrawolly,) with some account of their nature and contents.

In consequence of these interesting communications, applications have been repeatedly made by the writer for specimens of negro writings; and ~~a few months ago~~ he received, from President Benson and ex-President Roberts, several manuscripts of considerable length, written with neatness, uniformity, and elegance, which excite admiration. The compositions are original, having been written at Monrovia, at the request of those distinguished gentlemen, by accomplished negro Mohammedan travellers on visits there from the interior. They have been translated by the Rev. Dr. Bird, of Hartford, and contain evidence of a sincere religious zeal in the writers, who address their solemn appeals to the unknown stranger who had requested a written communication from them, presuming, as it appears, that he was not a Moslem, and was, therefore, ignorant of his Maker, his obligations to him, and the importance of knowing and serving him. Some passages in ~~those documents would~~ be perfectly appropriate to a sermon, even in an American pulpit, except that the idea of a Saviour is not expressed; but there are other parts which display the extreme ignorance of the writers respecting countries distant from their own. One of the manuscripts gives a description of China, full of the greatest extravagance, showing a degree of childish misconception and credulity which might be thought a proof of negro mental imbecility had we not in our hands Sir John Maundeville's Travels. That book, which was most extensively read in various languages in Europe four centuries ago, contains descriptions and pictures of men with two heads, and various other monsters, reported to be the inhabitants of fabulous countries, or lands barely known by name.

The following interesting account we copy from the Rev. William Fox's History of the Wesleyan Missions in Western Africa, page 462. It relates incidents of his journey to Footah-Bundu, where he attempted to establish a mission. That is the part of the country where "Old Paul" completed his education. On arriving at Jumé, he says it is a Serrawolly (or Sereculy) town, "somewhat noted as being the residence of a Marraboo priest, named Kabba, who has scholars from different parts of the country. He was busy with his pupils, but immediately came to give us a hearty welcome, and soon after he sent me three fowls. Here our guide gave a history of our proceedings from Kanipe to this place. After he had done the priest commenced a prayer for us; the people, with their hands upon their foreheads, as on former occasions, saying, at the end of every sentence, 'Amín! amín!'"

On the next day, which was Sunday, Mr. Fox says "The priest was busy all the day, so that I had not an opportunity of speaking to him until the evening, when I presented him with a handsomely bound Arabic Testament, and held a lengthy conversation with him on the subject of experimental religion, in the presence of a large congregation."

The next day, continues the narrator, "we rose early, and went to the priest to procure a guide. . . . Soon after the interview I accompanied the Mohammedan scribe to see his brother, who was sick, at whose request I prayed. . . . This place is one of the strongholds of the Mohammedan creed. . . . A little before five P. M., the guide being ready, I immediately mounted, and we were in the act of starting; but the priest thought proper to give us his blessing, which he did by taking hold of my hands while on horseback, and saying something which I did not understand; but the people around us were all attention, and they stood with both their hands open, as if they expected something to fall from the clouds at the close of the ceremony; and, as before, they all said, *Amín! amín!* We now proceeded, upward of one hundred of the inhabitants, men, women, and children, following us, sometimes completely surrounding my horse, wishing me to shake hands with them. I did so until I was tired, and ultimately was obliged to gallop off."

The following passages from the Arabic manuscripts above referred to will interest the reader. They are

extracts from Dr. Bird's translation of an Arabic
manuscript, written in Monrovia, by a negro from the
interior, at the request of President Benson, of Liberia, for a gentleman in New York. The manuscript
begins, like the chapters of the Koran, and all common Arab writings, with these words : "In the name
of God, the compassionate, the merciful," and adds :
"May God bless our lord Mohammed, his prophet,
and guard him and his disciples, and give him peace
abundantly." Then follow several pages on "the
Origin of Man," in which the creative power and the
wisdom and benevolence of God are magnified; after
which the writer proceeds thus :

And God said : "O children of Adam, when you arrive at
the age of ten you are bordering on the years to men and women, and you will be expected to attend prayers and preaching, and bear testimony, and not fear the Day of Judgment.
You will be tempted by men, who will say : Pursue the ways
of sin and disobedience and forgetfulness of what I, the Merciful, have enjoined upon you times without number. O man
of thirty years, reckon not yourself a little child, but a man
grown. Attend to your fasts, your prayers, day and night ;
and, if you continue thus day and night, you will be reckoned
among the excellent of men, being, in secret and before the
world, the same. Son of Adam, if you have come to forty
years you have attained your full strength. The marks of full
age bear witness to this ; your vigor is ripe, your mind is mature ; what you have learned is written well on your memory.
Guard against wine, and the indulgence of impurity. And then,
thou son of fifty years, thou knowest the advantages thy love
to the faith hath procured thee. It has brought thee into the
society of the great, and it has pleased Him who is the possessor of all excellency and power. Thou son of sixty years,
from the decline of your strength your passions are cooled.
Look at your noon of life, and judge how far your life and

death are in your power ; and, if you have not given up your hope in the word of God's prophet, (may God bless him !) you will have established for yourself a good household in these sixty years. O ye who heed not what shall come upon you, take care how you put any one in partnership with God ; for this is a dangerous sin, like that of the spilling of blood. O thou son of seventy years, estimate not yourself from the length of your past life, but from the nearness of your death. O thou man of ninety, death is coming upon you with power ; but there is no pain in Paradise. O man of a hundred, worn out with a hundred cares ; thou who hast challenged to thyself the age of Noah, peace be on thee ! Alas ! alas ! how wilt thou meet thy reward and thy Rewarder ? The Most High has brought your stewardship to a close, according to the word of the Lord, who thus testifies to every man who has a heart and an ear : 'O ye old men, remember that the seed, after it has sprouted forth, and before the harvest, dies.' O ye young people, how many that began life have been removed before growing up ! Where are Charon and his host ? They have perished. Where are Shadad-ibn-Aad and his host ? They have perished. Where are Pharaoh, the accursed, and his host ? They have perished. Where are Nimrod, son of Canaan, and his host ? Where are the sons and daughters, fathers and mothers of the past idolaters ? All perished. Where are your own fathers and mothers, ancient and modern ? They also have all perished ; and be assured that your end will be the same as theirs."

This passage in the manuscript is followed by several pages of fabulous names and dates, professing to be historical, and extravagant accounts of animals, the heavenly bodies, etc., in which mystical numbers are connected with childish errors and impossible events in great confusion. It would seem as if the author had endeavored to write on different subjects of which he once had read or heard, but, being far

3*

from his books, remembered correctly only the religious doctrines, which had made a clearer impression on his mind.

The following are extracts from the translation of a manuscript received from ex-President Roberts. This also is written with great elegance and correctness, the proper names being in red ink, and the points carefully marked. This manuscript occupies sixteen letter-sheet pages ; the other, eighteen.

In the name of God, most merciful and gracious, may God bless our lord Mohammed.

Thanks be to God, who is worthy of all gratitude and praise, the forgiver of sins, the possessor of the throne of glory, who created all things by himself, who created death and life, and created the earth and the heavens, and made all creatures in heaven and in the earth, who made the race of man from water ; then he made the blood, the heart, and the bones, then he spread the flesh upon the bones, then he added the tendons. Then said God, (be he exalted,) who created you from the ground and from water, that we might show and confirm through mercy what we wish to every generation. . . . O ye people, know ye that God is merciful toward you ; but that coming day will be terrible to the unbelievers, who live not as though there were a God, nor as if we were going to return to him. . . . O ye people, fear God and serve your Lord. Do your good works before the dissolution of death. . . . That day, God has said, nothing will profit you but a pure heart. . Beware, yea, beware, lest you hear the truth without repenting, and thus debase yourself. If you are asleep, be aroused ; if you are ignorant, make inquiry ; if you are forgetful, refresh your memory ; for here are the learned, ready to instruct you ; and, said he, on whom be peace, seek after knowledge. Well then, you may say, for example, give us a description of China, ye men of knowledge.

China.—China is a distant country, so that, though you

have shoes of iron, they would be worn out before you reach
it. The name of the Sultan is Aivor. It is said that the
journey between Medina and China is one of five years.
Some say five hundred years. There are in China ten mountains. • One of them has on it two trees, one of which can cover
all the people of the country with its shadow; at the same
time, if a single man seeks a shelter under it, the shadow cov-
ers him and no more. . . . In China are found two kettles, in
one of which they cook for all the inhabitants of the country,
and they all eat their fill, and there is none too much. In the
other they do cooking for strangers if they come among them,
and they eat and are satisfied, and there is nothing over.
There are in China two serpents, etc., etc.

After a few more such remarkable and incredible
statements, the writer says:

This account of China may possibly be considered a blemish
on this book ; but such is the character of the country, on the
authority of the learned.

He then commences a long and solemn appeal to
the unknown person in whose name he had been requested to send something in writing, and whom he
appears to have supposed to be ignorant of the first
principles of religion, but for whom he feels an affec-
tionate regard.

O my brother's son, do not join yourself with Satan, for Satan is your enemy, as God, the exalted, has said—for Satan is
your enemy ; and will you make partnership with your enemy ? . . . O, my brother's son, let not the affairs of this life
draw away your affections. Follow not the wind ; do not deceive yourself, but be prepared, before sickness, or poverty,
or old age engross your attention. God, the exalted, says,
O man ! who has set you against your Lord, who created,
shaped, and adjusted you, and put you together in the form
that pleased him ? God, the exalted, says that the life of this
world is of very little profit in the world to come.

The following are extracts from a letter sent to " Old Paul" by a venerable old slave, long known at Fayetteville, N. C., and there called " Morro," in reply to one addressed to him, in 1836 :

In the name of God, the compassionate, etc. I am not able to write my life. I have forgotten much of the language of the Arabs. I read not the grammatical, but little of the common dialect. I ask thee, O brother, to reproach me not, for my eyes are weak, and my body also. [He was then about seventy-one years of age.]

My name is Omar-ben-Sayeed. The place of my birth is Footah-Toro, between the two rivers. [Probably the Senegal and Gambia, or the Senegal and Niger, in their upper parts.] The teachers of Bundu-foota were a sheik, named Mohammed-Sayeed, my brother, and the sheik Soleyman Kimba, and the sheik Jebraeel-Abdel. I was teacher twenty-five years. There came a great army to my country. They killed many people. They took me to the sea, and sold me in the hands of the Christians, who bound me, and sent me on board of a great ship. And we sailed a month and a half a month, when we came to a place called Charlestown in the Christian language. Here they sold me to a small, weak, and wicked man named Johnson, a complete infidel, who had no fear of God at all. Now I am a small man, and not able to do hard work. So I fled from the hands of Johnson, and, after a month, came to a place where I saw some houses. On the new moon I went into a large house to pray ; a lad saw me, and rode off to the place of his father, and informed him that he had seen a black man in the great house. A man named Handah (Hunter,) and another man with him, on horseback, came, attended by a troop of dogs. They took me and made me go with them twelve miles, to a place called Faydill, (Fayetteville,) where they put me in a great house, from which I could not go out. I continued in the great house, which in the Christian language they call *jail*, sixteen days and nights. One Friday the jailer came and opened the door, and I saw a great many men, all of them Christians, some of whom called out, What is your name ? I did not understand their Chris tian language.

A man called Bob Mumford took me and led me out of the jail, and I was very well pleased to go with them to their place. I staid at Mumford's four days and nights, and then a man named Jim Owen, son-in-law of Mumford, who married his daughter Betsey, asked me if I was willing to go to a place called Bladen. I said yes, I was willing. I went with them, and have remained on the place of Jim Owen until now.

O people of North Carolina ! O people of South Carolina ! O people of America, all of you ! you have a righteous man among you named James Owen, and with him John Owen. These are pious men. All that they eat I ate ! as they dressed I dressed. James and his brother read to me the Gospel. God our Lord, our Creator, our King, the arbiter of our condition, the bountiful, opened to my heart the right way.

The translator remarked as follows on the style of writing in the manuscript.

The narrative is very obscure in language, the writer, as he himself declares, being ignorant of the grammatical forms. . . It is written in a plain and, with few exceptions, very legible *Moghrebby*, or western Arabic character. . . . It affords an idea of the degree of education among the Moslem blacks, when we see a man like this able to read and write a language so different from his own native tongue. Where is the youth, or even the adult, among the mass of our people, who is able to do the same in Latin or Greek ?

By a fortunate incident the writer of one of the first-mentioned manuscripts from Liberia, added at the end half a page in some language unknown to the translator ; but doubtless some African tongue ; thus affording evidence of the interesting fact, so little known in our country, that native languages are written in Arabic characters.

IV.

CONDITION OF EDUCATION IN LIBERIA.

LETTERS from leading men in Liberia in 1867 and 1868 having represented that great numbers of colonists had come there from the United States, and were still coming, without any more education than the heathen natives, and that they were entirely destitute of the means of providing schools, and that the government was unable to help them; while great disaster threatened the country unless some provision was made for educating them, in the Autumn of 1868 the New York State Colonization Society sent out its Corresponding Secretary, Rev. J. B. Pinney, D.D., who had during the last thirty years visited Liberia three or four times. Dr. Pinney made an exploration so thorough, that, as Professor Blyden wrote, he must be the best authority for years to come as to the condition of Liberia. Dr. Pinney found less than thirty schools, averaging not over twenty scholars each, to supply a population of five or six hundred thousand, natives and Americans, or about one scholar to every one thousand inhabitants. As Secretary of the New York State Colonization Society, he has, since his return, been exerting himself to supply schools, and has succeeded in organizing fourteen small ones during the last year, at a cost of about one hundred and fifty

dollars each, without, however, having secured any permanent means for their continuance.

Except the missions of the American churches, to
which Liberia is indebted for the few schools which Dr.
Pinney found there, he is alone in this effort, and should
he discontinue it, what is to prevent the rising generation from growing up as ignorant as their parents;
than which nothing could more endanger the success
and stability of the Republic.

Isaac J. Smith, Esq., President of the Metropolitan
Savings Bank, No 1. Third Avenue, New York, is the
Treasurer of the New York State Colonization Society,
and contributions for the support of these schools will
be received by him, or the Rev. J. B. Pinney, D.D.,
22 Bible House, New York.

V.

EXTRACTS FROM PROF. BLYDEN'S JOURNAL OF A

VISIT TO SIERRA LEONE IN FEBRUARY, 1871.

Monday, 16.—This morning I transferred myself and
young Warner, my *protegé*, to the Grammar School.
I am now comfortably, or rather congenially, located,
with a large library around me, and a learned negro to
converse with.   Mr. Quaker was born in Sierra Leone,
of native parents, and educated partly at Fourah Bay,
under Rev. E. Jones, and partly in England.   He has
been in charge of the Grammar School for twenty
years, and has turned out, he informed me, over a
thousand scholars.   He now has about one hundred

pupils—all, with one or two exceptions, pure negroes ; and a more orderly school, and a more intelligent and sprightly set of boys, I never saw.

After leaving the Grammar School, I went to the Post-office. On my way thence I met a learned Mandingo, very black, who spoke Arabic fluently. He was quite surprised at my speaking it. He asked me where I learned it. I told him principally from books, but that I had spent three months in the East. He followed me to my rooms, and we had a very interesting time together. He told me that he had himself travelled as far as Egypt and Jerusalem—" *Beni Israel*," as he called the Holy City. He spoke of the Mosque of Omar and the Mosque El-Aksa. After he left, my fame went abroad as an Arabic scholar (an alleged philological eminence which I sometimes regretted, though in some instances it was of great service to me, and perhaps to the cause of truth). In the evening a young man of Aku parentage, who spoke Arabic fluently, called upon me. He was born in Sierra Leone, but has travelled in the interior as far as Futa. He sat with me about one hour, conversing and reading Arabic.

Thursday, 12.—To-day called upon the Chief-Justice at the Barracks, who received me very courteously. He is a large, burly Englishman. He said he had been in the colony four years, and had not had one day's illness; that he had abstained altogether from the use of brandy, &c.

Friday, 13.—To-day spent most of the day at home, preparing to lecture this evening. At 7 o'clock P. M., a number of gentlemen called to accompany me to the lecture. They sold tickets—price sixpence each. The Court Hall was nearly crowded. I lectured on "Mohammedanism in Western Africa." There were two learned Mohammedans present, and they seemed quite interested, as they understood both the English and my Arabic quotations and recitations from the Koran.

Saturday, 14.—After breakfast I walked out to visit the market, which is unusually full and crowded on Saturdays. I saw hundreds of people from the neighboring villages selling. After breakfast I walked out for exercise, and met a tall, portly Mandingo, with flowing robe of spotless white, followed by a train of carriers, bearing hides. I went up and saluted him in Arabic. He looked at me with an air of surprise, and for a few seconds made me no reply. I addressed him again. He asked, "Where did you learn Arabic?" I told him. I asked him where he was from? He replied Timbuctu (Timbuctoo). I asked him if he knew Kankan and Musardu and Madina. He said yes—that he sometimes went to Musardu to trade; and he pointed to persons among his followers from different towns in the interior.

VI.

THE SYRIAN (Arabic) COLLEGE.

As has already been stated, Professor Blyden visited the Syrian Protestant College at Beirut, in 1866, for the purpose of perfecting his knowledge of the Arabic language. Previous to his visit, the Rev. Daniel Bliss, D.D., the president of the institution, had sent to Liberia for distribution, in the interior, a number of volumes, on the fly leaves of which he had written in Arabic certain queries, and requesting answers to them. They will be found in Mr. Blyden's account of the Arabic manuscript of Ibrahima Kaba-wee. The following brief account of the Syrian College, cannot fail to command the attention of those interested in the work of modern missions.

It is located in Beirut, the chief seaport of Syria, a city of 80,000 inhabitants, growing in size and importance, and occupying a central position in respect to all the Arabic-speaking races. Planted at such a centre, the college will not only become a power in moulding the literary character and promoting the religious advancement of Syria, but will naturally extend its blessings to the populations of the adjoining countries.

The college is incorporated in accordance with the laws of the State of New York. A preparatory department was established in 1865, the regular course was begun in the autumn of the following year, and the medical department added one year later.

The language of the college is exclusively Arabic, the common tongue of Syria, and used by more than one hundred millions of people throughout the East. The course of instruction embraces the several branches of the Arabic language and literature, mathematics, the natural sciences, modern languages, Turkish, English, French and Latin, moral science, Biblical literature, and the various departments of medicine and surgery, in connection with which there is established a hospital, with dispensary and pharmacy, where more than five thousand cases have been treated, in most instances gratuitously.

The institution is under the general control of trustees in the United States, where the present funds are invested, but local affairs are administered by a board of managers, composed of American and British missionaries, and residents in Syria and Egypt.

The college is conducted upon strictly Protestant and Evangelical principles, but is open to students from any of the Oriental sects and nationalities who will conform to its regulations. More than eighty young men are now enjoying the advantages it offers.

The sects now represented are the Protestant, Orthodox-Greek, Papal-Greek, Latin, Maronite, Druze, Armenian, and Coptic. Direct proselytism is not attempted ; but, without endeavoring to force Protestantism upon students of other sects, every effort is made by the personal intercourse of professors and

instructors, in the class-room and at other times, and
by the general exercises and arrangements of the
institution, to bring each member into contact with the
distinctive features of Evangelical truth. All boarders
are required to be present at both morning and evening prayers, to attend Protestant worship and college
Bible classes upon the Sabbath, and a recitation of
the Scriptures or Biblical lectures during the week.
The Bible is also used as a text-book for ordinary
instruction. A voluntary weekly prayer-meeting has
been carried on by the students, and several are
engaged in Evangelical work in the city.

A text book on Chemistry, and portions of a general
work on Natural History have lately been published,
and one on Anatomy is now in press. These books are
illustrated. Works on Physiology, Pathology, Diseases of the Skin, Natural and Mental Philosophy, and
higher mathematics, are ready for printing or in
course of preparation, all in the Arabic language.

Prof. D. Stuart Dodge, recently returned from Syria,
is authorized to represent the interests of the college.

Its Board of Trustees are:

New York.
- WILLIAM A. BOOTH, *President.*
- HON. WILLIAM E. DODGE, *Treasurer.*
- DAVID HOADLEY.
- SIMEON B. CHITTENDEN.

Boston.
- ABNER KINGMAN.
- JOSEPH S. ROPES.

VII.

ARABIC MANUSCRIPT IN WESTERN AFRICA.

THE history and translation of the Arabic manuscript of which an exact fac simile copy, taken by photographic process, is annexed, will be found in the following extract of a letter from Professor Blyden to Mr. H. M. Schieffelin, of New York, dated,

MONROVIA, *Dec.* 7, 1870.

"You will be gratified to learn that at the examination of the Senior Class, which took place on the 25th ult., there was present a learned Muslim from Kankan, who had come in to visit me a few days previously.

I invited him to attend the Senior examination. He came with his numerous manuscripts and took his seat among the examiners, between Professor Johnson and myself. When the Arabic class came forward, he seemed very much interested. After answering several preliminary questions on the history and sacred language of the Mohammedans, the students recited from memory passages from various parts of the Koran in Arabic. Whenever they would begin a passage, he would turn at once to it in a MS. Koran, which he had at his side. The students then read one of the Makamat of Hariri in the original (De Sacy's edition). Our Mohammedan visitor happened to have with him the whole of the fifty Makamat in elegant manuscript. He followed the students as they read, repeating after them in an undertone. Of course he could not judge of the translation, as he understood not a word of English. I communicated with him in Arabic. After the students had read I requested him to read the same portion, that they might hear his pronunciation. He read in the musical cantilating manner of the East, and the listener who had travelled in these countries might have fancied himself on the banks of the Nile, or on Mount Lebanon.

It is now certain that Liberia College and the work that we are attempting to do here for Africa are known in the far interior, among the Arabic reading population : and by a little energetic management on our part it would be comparatively easy to establish regular intercourse between our schools and the schools of Misádu, Mediva, Kankan and Futah. Such relations would result in great good to our little republic, and to this portion of Africa.

A few years ago—perhaps in 1864—Rev. Daniel Bliss, D.D., President of the Syrian Protestant College, at Beirut, sent to Liberia College several Arabic books printed in Syria for distribution among the Arabic reading people accessible to Liberia. On a blank leaf in each of the volumes was printed an Arabic letter, addressed "From the city of Beirut, in the country of Syria, to the noble lords living in Central Africa," proposing certain questions and requesting answers to them.

. Some time ago I met a Mandingo priest—Kaifal—

at Vonzwah, and requested him to write answers to the questions. He complied with my request, but only partially. I gave a book containing the questions to my recent guest, and requested written answers from him : after reading them over carefully once or twice, he produced, *calamo currente*, the paper which I enclose herewith, and of which I send you a translation.

The paper sent from Beirut I have translated as follows :

From the city of Beirut, in the country of Syria, to the noble lords living in Central Africa. Peace to all.

O YE NOBLE LORDS !

We have learned of the existence of tribes south of the great desert, whose dialect is the noble Arabic language, and that they extend from there to the central countries of Africa. As we desire information respecting them, we have taken this method for that purpose, hoping that whoever may chance to receive this paper will favor us with answers to the subjoined questions, by the hand of the head of the College of Liberia, which country is west from your country, as we have understood. By this means you will establish a connection between yourselves and the learned men of the College of Beirut, and the chief of its printing department; and this may be an advantage to you.

What is your religion ?

What is the number of your people ?

Is there unity among the tribes whose language is the Arabic, or are they divided into separate communities ?

Are they all under one government ?

Where is its seat or capital ?

Are all the Arabic tribes in your country of one religion ?

What is the extent of your country ?

Are there among you many books—what are the names of the principal and most valuable ones ?

Are there among you any authors—on what subjects have they written ?

REPLY.

By Ibrahima Kabwee, a Native of Kankan.

In the name of God, the Merciful, the Gracious. God bless our Lord Mohammed, his prophet, and his family, and his companions, and keep them safe.

The learned men in our country Africa, to the learned men in Beirut, in the country of Syria.   Peace to all.

O ye Noble Lords !

Your letter and your questions have reached us, and we desire to send you answers to your questions.

You ask, "What is your religion ?" Our religion is the religion of Islam. The number of our people is very, very great, and we are not divided into separate portions. We are all under one rule, and we belong to the sect of the Malikees.[1] Our religion and the religion of the Arab is one religion. The extent of our country is from Rokoma (Boporo) to Soudan ; and from Misādu, and Mediva, and Kankan, and Futah, and Hamd-Allahi, and Jenne, and Timbuktu—all these cities have one religion.

There are many books in our country, and the names of these books are, the *Makamat,* and all the Makamat are fifty; and the name of the author of the *Makamat* is Abu Kasim Al-Hariri ; and another book is the *Risālat.* The author of the *Risālat* is Abu Mohammed Salihu ; and the *Tawhid,* and *Loghat,* and *Tasrif,* and the *Kamus,* and the *Koran,* and *Jalaludin.* But the Koran is the chief of all books ; men know it and do not know it ; they see it and do not see it ; they hear it and do not hear it.

There are many authors among us, and they have written the encomiums of the prophet of God—the *Bunmuhaib,* the *Watirati,* the *Salat Rabbe,* and the *Shifaee,* and the *Tanbihu-*

---

[1] The Mohammedans are divided into four parties or persuasions— the "Hanafees," "Shafees," "Malikees" and "Hambalees," so called from the names of the respective doctors whose tenets they have adopted.

كثير واسمه بلده موه وامام كنها كنها ابوبكر شريه
وفي بلد ذا هال كثير والناس كثير مسلمين كاهم
والتمر والعماره والبعد والخار والمعزو الدجا
جة وذا هب واللخصة وكالهم كثير وبلد
كنك المسيرة من مساد الى كنها تسع
ايام وفي لمريو الكفار كثير ومسيرة من
كنك الوقوتي مساد سر ايام ملك كنها
ها بعي وملك مدينته ملك وملد
مساد سر ما ير المسلمين والكفار و ولد
وملك بحكم كا بر عظيم اسمه
سا بنر ونفذ الحمد لله رب العلمين

﴿ اسمه صادبه عبد الكريم
واسم خطه ابراهيم كبوى
س الامين وامه داسكبوى ﴾

يسلم اسم بلد ذا اسم ملها كنك كنت محمود شا فعى

ومحمود ثاء العلم والعرب واسم شيخ محمود

الحجم والحجم ذاهب الومك وحجا ومرو ومدينه

وشام ومصر ورجع الحجم الى تنبت ومضى مرتبت

الوحمد الله ومضى مر حمد الله الى سجد رومضى

مر سجار الوجر ومضى جر الوكنك والمولبون

المولود في بلا دنا كنك ابو شيخنا اسمه محمد

شريف وهو مولف الكتب اثير واسم الخبير

روضه سعاده ومعد رذاهب وشيخنا اسمه

ابو بكر شريف وهو مولف الكتب واحد اسم

الكتب ذا الى صغير وعمر الكدار وهو مولف الكتب

كثير الكتب في بلدانها واسمي كتبنا مقامات ومقام
كلهم خمسون ومقامات اسم مؤلف مقام ابو الفلسم
الحريري ورسالة اسم مؤلف رسال ابو محمد صالح
وتوحيد وفقه واللغة وتصريف وقاموس والد
القرى اروالجلال ويرو القرء ان سيد الكتب كلهم
يعرف الناس ولا يعرف الناس ييسر ولا ييسر
يسمع ولا يسمع مولى عندنا كثير ويولى بور
مدح نبى الله بمهيب والوتريات وصلاة
رب وما تار وشهدا وتنبيه الانام ودلام الخيرات
كلهم مدح نبى الله هو ذاك سيد الورى وسيد
تقلين الانس والجن محمد رسول الله صلى الله عليه

بسم الله الرحمن الرحيم صلى الله على سيدنا
محمد نبيه وعلى آله وصحبه وسلم تسليما العلماء
في بلدتنا الفرقية الى العلماء في بيروت في بر الشام
كل سلام ايها السادة الكرام وصلتنا رسالاتكم
ومسائلكم واردة نائر سلو عليكم بجواب للمسائل
اولا ما هو مذاهبكم ومنذ كم نحن ادير الاسلام عدد
نفومنا كثير جدا اكثير اجدا الانفسهم احزاب احزابا
هل جميعهم تحت حكم واحد و ديانتنا مالكي مذاهبنا
ومذاهب العرب دير واحد حداود امر بعضهم الى
السدار ومرمسادومه يناولكنك وبوتووا الحمد
الله وجروت تنبت دير واحد هذا المدينة كلهم

al-Anam, and the *Dalail-al-Kheirāti*. All these are concerning the prophet of God, who is the chief of creatures, the lord of men, of demons and of genii—Mohammed, the Apostle of God. (God bless him, and grant him peace.)

The name of our town is Kankan, the name of the king of Kankan is Mahmud, and he is a Shafee by sect; Mahmud is skilled in literature and in war. And the name of the Sheikh of Mahmud is Al-hajj. He went on a pilgrimage to Mecca, and Lafa, and Merwa, and Mediva, and Syria, and Egypt. Then the pilgrim returned to Timbuktu, and journeyed from Timbuktu to Hamd-Allahi, and from Hamd-Allahi to Sōfāla, and from Sōfāla to Jenne, and from Jenne to Kankan.

The authors born in our town Kankan, are : our Sheikh, Mohammed Shereef. He is the author of two books, and the names of the books are : *Rawdat Saadat* (the Garden of Delight), and *Maadan Zahab* (The Mine of Gold) ; and our Sheikh, Abubeker Shereef. He is the author of one book, and the name of his book is *Dalya Saghir ;* and Amru Alkidi. He is the author of many books ; the name of his town is Mowa. The Imam of Kankan is Abubeker Shereef.

In our town is much wealth, and the inhabitants are all Muslims. And there are horses, and asses, and mules, and sheep, and goats, and fowls, and gold, and silver, all in great abundance in the town of Kankan.

The journey from Misādu to Kankan is nine days, and on the road are many pagans ; and the journey from Kankan to Futah is six days. The King of Kankan is a Shafee by sect. The King of Misādu is partly Moslem and partly pagan. The King of Bokoma is a great pagan, his name is Labsu Mohammed. Praise be to God, the Lord of the three worlds.

The name of the writer of this is Ibrahima Kabawee.

4

VIII.
MOHAMMEDANISM IN WESTERN AFRICA.

From the Methodist Quarterly Review, January, 1871.

BY REV. E. W. BLYDEN.

PROFESSOR OF LANGUAGES, IN LIBERIA COLLEGE.

GEORGE SALE has prefixed to the title-page of his able translation of the Koran the following motto from Saint Augustin : " *Nulla falsa doctrina est, quae non aliquid veri permisceat.*" Recent discussions and investigations have brought the subject of Mohammedanism prominently before the reading public, and the writings of Weil, and Nöldeke, and Muir, and Sprenger, and Emanuel Deutsch have taught the world that " Mohammedanism is a thing of vitality, fraught with a thousand fruitful germs ;" and have amply illustrated the principle enunciated by Saint Augustin, showing that there *are* elements both of truth and goodness in a system which has had so wide-spread an influence upon mankind, embracing within the scope of its operations more than one hundred millions of the human race ; that the exhibition of gems of truth, even though " suspended in a gallery of counterfeits," has vast power over the human heart.

The object of the present paper is to inquire briefly

into the condition and influence of Mohammedanism among the tribes of Western Africa. Whatever may be the intellectual inferiority of the negro tribes, (if, indeed, such inferiority exists,) it is certain that many of these tribes have received the religion of Islam without its being forced upon them by the overpowering arms of victorious invaders. The quiet development and organization of a religious community in the heart of Africa has shown that negroes, equally with other races, are susceptible of moral and spiritual impressions, and of all the sublime possibilities of religion. The history of the progress of Islam in this country would present the same instances of real and eager mental conflict, of minds in honest transition, of careful comparison and reflection, that have been found in other communities where new aspects of truth and fresh considerations have been brought before them. And we hold that it shows a stronger and more healthy intellectual tendency to be induced by the persuasion and reason of a man of moral nobleness and deep personal convictions to join with him in the introduction of beneficial changes, than to be compelled to follow the lead of an irresponsible character who forces us into measures by his superior physical might.

Different estimates are made of the beneficial effects wrought by Islam upon the moral and industrial condition of Western Africa. Some are disposed to ignore altogether any wholesome result, and regard the negro Moslems as possessing as a general thing only the external appendages of a system which they do not understand. But such a conclusion implies a

very superficial acquaintance with the state of things
among the people. Of course cases are found of
individuals here and there, of blustering zeal and
lofty pretensions—qualities which usually exist in
inverse proportion to the amount of sound knowledge
possessed—whose views, so far as they can be gathered, are no more than a mixture of imperfectly
understood Mohammedanism and fetichism; but all
careful and candid observers agree that the influence
of Islam in Central and West Africa has been, upon
the whole, of a most salutary character. As an eliminatory and subversive agency, it has displaced or
unsettled nothing as good as itself. If it has introduced superstitions, it has expelled superstitions far
more mischievous and degrading. And it is not
wonderful if, in succeeding to a debasing heathenism,
it has in many respects made compromises, so as
occasionally to present a barren hybrid character.
But what *is* surprising is that a religion quietly introduced from a foreign country, with so few of the
outward agencies of civilization, should not in process
of time have been altogether absorbed by the superstitions and manners of barbarous pagans. But not
only has it not been absorbed, it has introduced large
modifications in the views and practices even of those
who have but a vague conception of its teachings.

Mungo Park, in his travels seventy years ago,
everywhere remarked the contrast between the pagan
and Mohammedan tribes of interior Africa. One
very important improvement noticed by him was
abstinence from intoxicating drinks. "The beverage of
the pagan negroes," he says, "is *beer and mead*, of

which they often drink to excess; the Mohammedan
converts drink *nothing but water.*" [1] Thus throughout
Central Africa there has been established a vast *total
abstinence society;* and such is the influence of this
society, that where there are Moslem inhabitants, even
in pagan towns, it is a very rare thing to see a person
intoxicated. They thus present an almost impene-
trable barrier to the desolating flood of ardent spirits
with which traders from Europe and America inundate
the coast, and of which we have recently had so
truthful and sadly suggestive an account from a
missionary at Gaboon. [2]

Wherever the Moslem is found on this coast,
whether Jalof, Foulah, or Mandingo, he looks upon
himself as a separate and distinct being from his
pagan neighbor, and immeasurably his superior in
intellectual and moral respects. He regards himself
as one to whom a revelation has been " sent down "
from heaven. He holds constant intercourse with the
" Lord of worlds," whose servant he is. In his behalf Omnipotence will ever interpose in times of
danger. Hence he feels that he cannot indulge in the
frivolities and vices which he considers as by no
means incompatible with the character and professions
of the Kafir or unbeliever. Nearly every day his
Koran reminds him of his high privileges, as compared
with others, in the following terms :

Verily those who believe not, among those have received the
Scriptures, and among the idolaters, shall be cast into the fire
of hell, to remain therein forever. These are the worst of

[1] Park's Travels, chap. ii.
[2] Mr. Walker, in " Miss. Herald," Feb. 1870.

creatures. But they who believe and do good works, these are
the best of creatures; their reward with their Lord shall be
gardens of perpetual abode.[1]

Whoso taketh God and his apostle and the believers for
friends, they are the party of God, and they shall be victorious.[2]

But there are no caste distinctions among them.
They do not look upon the privileges of Islam as
confined by tribal barriers or limitations. On the
contrary, the life of their religion is aggressiveness.
They are constantly making proselytes. As early as
the commencement of the present century the elastic
and expansive character of their system was suffi-
ciently marked to attract the notice of Mr. Park.
"In the negro country," observes that celebrated
traveler, "the Mohammedan religion has made, *and
continues to make,* considerable progress." "The
yearning of the native African," says Professor
Crummel, "for a higher religion, is illustrated by the
singular fact that Mohammedanism is rapidly and
peaceably spreading all through the tribes of Western
Africa, even to the Christian settlements of Liberia."[3]
From Senegal to Lagos, over two thousand miles,
there is scarcely an important town on the sea-board
where there are not at least one mosque and active
representatives of Islam, often side by side with the
Christian teacher. And as soon as a pagan, however
obscure or degraded, embraces the Moslem faith, he
is at once admitted as an equal to their society.
Slavery and the slave-trade are laudable institutions,
provided the slaves are Kafirs. The slave who

[1] Sura xciii.   [2] Sura v.

[3] "Future of Africa," p. 305.

embraces Islam is free, and no office is closed against him on account of servile blood.

The pagan village possessing a Mussulman teacher is always found to be in advance of its neighbors in all the elements of civilization. The people pay great deference to him. He instructs their children, and professes to be the medium between them and heaven, either for securing a supply of their necessities, or for warding off or removing calamities. It must be borne in mind that people in the state of barbarism in which the pagan tribes are usually found have no proper conceptions of humanity and its capacities. The man, therefore, who by unusual strength or cunning achieves something which no one had achieved before him, or of which they do not understand the process, is exalted into an extraordinary being, in close intimacy with the mysterious powers of nature. The Mohammedan, then, who enters a pagan village with his books and papers and rosaries, his frequent ablutions and regularly recurring times of prayers and prostrations, in which he appears to be conversing with some invisible being, soon acquires a controlling influence over the people. He secures their moral confidence and respect, and they bring to him all their difficulties for solution and all their grievances for redress.

To the African Mussulman, innocent of the intellectual and scientific progress of other portions of the world, the Koran is all-sufficient for his moral, intellectual, social and political needs. It contains his whole religion and a great deal besides. It is to him far more than it is to the Turk or Egyptian upon whom the light of European civilization has fallen. It is his code of laws and his creed, his homily and his liturgy. He consults it for direction on every possible subject; and his pagan neighbor, seeing such veneration paid to the book, conceives even more exaggerated notions of its character. The latter looks upon it as a great medical repository, teaching the art of healing diseases, and as a wonderful storehouse of charms and divining power, protecting from dangers and foretelling future events. And though the prognostications of his Moslem prophet are often of the nature of *vaticinia post eventum*, yet his faith remains unshaken in the infallibility of "Alkorana." He, therefore, never fails to resort in times of extremity to the Mohammedan for direction, and pays him for charms against evil. These charms are nothing more than passages from the Koran written on slips of paper and inclosed in leather cases about two or three inches square—after the manner of the Jewish phylactery—and worn about the neck or wrist. The passages usually written are the last two chapters of the Koran, known as the "Chapters of Refuge," because they begin, "Say, I take refuge," etc. In cases of internal complaints one or both of these chapters are written on certain leaves, of which a strong decoction is made, and the water administered to the patient. We have seen these two chapters written inside a bowl at Alexandria for medicinal purposes.

The Moslems themselves wear constantly about their persons certain texts from the Koran called *Ayát-el-hifz*, verses of protection or preservation, which are supposed to keep away every species of misfortune. The following are in most common use : " God is the best *protector*, and he is the most merciful of those who show mercy." (Sura xii. 64.) "And God compasseth them behind. Verily it is a glorious Koran, written on a *preserved* tablet," (Sura lxxxv. 20.) Sometimes they have the following rhymed couplet :

> Bismi illahi arrahman, arrahim
> Auzu billahi min es-Shaytan arrajim.[1]

This couplet is also employed whenever they are about to commence reading the Koran, as a protection against the suggestions of Satan, who is supposed to be ever on the alert to whisper erroneous and hurtful constructions to the devout reader.

The Koran is almost always in their hand. It seems to be their labor and their relaxation to pore over its pages. They love to read and recite it aloud for hours together. They seem to possess an enthusiastic appreciation of the rhythmical harmony in which it is written. But we cannot attribute its power over them altogether to the jingling sounds, wordplays, and refrains in which it abounds. These, it is true, please the ear and amuse the fancy, especially of the uncultivated. But there is something higher, of which these rhyming lines are the vehicle ; something possessing a deeper power to rouse the imagination, mold the feelings, and generate action. Mr. Gibbon has characterized the Koran as a " tissue of incoherent rhapsodies."[2] But the author of the "Decline and

---

[1] In the name of God, the Merciful, the Compassionate,
.I take refuge in God from Satan, whom we hate.
[2] Chap. 1.

4*

Fall" was, as he himself acknowledges, ignorant of the
Arabic language, and therefore incompetent to pronounce an authoritative judgment. Mr. Hallam, in a
more appreciative vein, speaks of it as "a book
confessedly written with much elegance and purity,"
containing "just and elevated notions of the divine
nature and moral duties, the gold ore that pervades
the dross." [1] The historian of the "Middle Ages," a
most conscientious investigator, had probably read the
book in the original—had been charmed with its *sense*
as well as its *sound*. Only they who read it in the
language of the Arabian author can form anything
like an accurate idea of its unapproachable place as a
power among unevangelized communities for molding
into the most exciting and the most expressive harmonies the feelings and imaginations. Says a recent
able and learned critic :

> The Koran suffers more than any other book we think of by
> a translation, however masterly. The grandeur of the Koran
> consists, its contents apart, in its diction. We cannot explain
> the peculiarly dignified, impressive, sonorous mixture of Se-
> mitic sound and parlance ; its *sesquipedalia verba*, with their
> crowd of prefixes and affixes, each of them affirming its own
> position, while consciously bearing upon and influencing the
> central root, which they envelop like a garment of many folds,
> or as chosen courtiers move round the anointed person of the
> King. [2]

The African Moslem forms no exception among the
adherents of Islam in his appreciation of the sacred
book. It is studied with as much enthusiam at

[1] "Middle Ages," chap. vi.
[2] Emanuel Deutsch, in the *Quarterly Review* (London) for October, 1869.

Boporo, Misadu, Medina, Kankan,[1] as at Cairo
Alexandria, or Bagdad. In travelling in the exterior
of Liberia we have met ulemas, or learned men, who
could reproduce from memory any chapter of the
Koran, with its vowels and dots and other grammatical marks. The boys under their instruction are
kept at the study of the books for years. First they
are taught the letters and vowel marks, then they are
taught to read the text without receiving any insight
into its meaning. When they can read fluently they
are taught the meaning of the words, which they
commit carefully to memory; after which they are
instructed in what they call the " Jatali," a running
commentary on the Koran. While learning the Jatali
they have side studies assigned them in Arabic
manuscripts, containing the mystical traditions, the
acts of Mohammed, the duties of fasting, prayer, alms,
corporal purification, etc.[2] Young men who intend to
be enrolled among the ulemas take up history and
chronology, on which they have some fragmentary
manuscripts. Before a student is admitted to the
ranks of the learned he must pass an examination,
usually lasting seven days, conducted by a Board
consisting of imáms and ulemas. If he is successful,
he is led around the town on horseback with instru-
mental music and singing. The following ditty is
usually sung:

[1] Mohammedan towns, from seventy-five to three hundred miles
east and north-east of Monrovia.

[2] The student at this stage is called tâlib, that is, *one who seeks
knowledge*.

Allahumma, ya Rabbee
Salla ala Mohammade,
Salla Allahu alayhe wa Sallama.[1]

After which the candidate is presented with a sash or scarf, usually of fine white cloth of native manufacture, which he is thenceforth permitted to wind round his cap, with one end hanging down the back, forming the Oriental turban. This is a sort of Bachelor of Arts diploma. The men who wear turbans have read and recited the Koran through many hundred times; and you can refer to no passage which they cannot readily find in their apparently confused manuscripts of loose leaves and pages, distinguished not by numbers, but by catch words at the bottom. Carlyle tells us that he has heard of Mohammedan doctors who had read the Koran seventy thousand times.[2] Many such animated and moving concordances to the Koran may doubtless be found in Central and West Africa.

But the Koran is not the only book they read. We have seen in some of their libraries extensive manuscripts in poetry and prose. One showed us at Boporo the *Makâmat* of Hariri, which he read and expounded with great readiness, and seemed surprised that we had heard of it. And it is not to be doubted that some valuable Arabic manuscripts may yet be found in the heart of Africa. Dr. Barth tells us that he saw in Central Africa a manuscript of those portions of Aristotle and Plato which had been translated into Arabic, and that an Arabic version of Hippo-

[1] O God, my Lord, bless Mohammed ! God bless him and grant him peace !

[2] "Heroes and Hero Worship," p. 80.

crates was extremely valued. The splendid voweled edition of the New Testament and Psalms recently issued by the American Bible Society, and of which, through the kindness of friends in New York, we have been enabled to distribute a few copies among them, is highly prized.

We have collected in our visits to Mohammedan towns a number of interesting manuscripts, original and extracted. We will here give two or three specimens as translated by us. We should be glad if we could transfer to these pages the elegant and ornamental chirography of the original.

The first is from a talismanic paper written at Futa Jallon, copies of which are sold to the credulous as means of warding off evil from individuals and communities, to be employed especially during seasons of epidemics. It is as follows:

In the name of God, the Merciful, the Compassionate. O God, bless Mohammed and save him, the seal of the prophets and the imâm of the apostles, beloved of the "Lord of worlds!"

After the above is the conveying of health, and the completing of salutation and honor.

Verily, the pestilence is coming upon you, beginning with your wealth, such as your cows, and after that upon yourselves ; and verily if all of you provide water and bread, namely, of your men and your women, and your man-servants and your maid-servants, and all your youths, they shall not endure it. And after that write out the Chapter *Opener of the Book*[1] and the *Verse of the Throne*,[2] and from "God is light" to "Omni-

[1] *Fatihat el-Kitab*, the first chapter of the Koran.
[2] *Ayet el-Kursee* Sura ii. iv. 256. This verse is repeated by the pious Moslem nearly every time he prays. It is as follows : "God !

scient," [1] and from "God created every," the whole verse to "Omnipotent," [2] and the *Two Chapters of Refuge;* and write, "They who when they have done foully and dealt unjustly by their own souls shall remember God, and seek forgiveness for their sins,' (and who forgives sins but God ?) and shall not persevere in what they have done while they know it." [3] And if you do this God shall certainly turn back the punishment from you, if God will, by this supplication. . . . Because that is the way of escape obligatory on every Moslem man and woman. This document is by a man of wealth, who traveled, traveling from Futa to Mecca on a pilgrimage, and stayed three months, and departed to El-Medina, and settled there three years, and returned to Futa. Written by me, Ahmad of Futa to-day. O God, bless Mohammed and save him ! The end."

The next paper professes to be a history of the world. Beginning thousands of years before Adam, it gives account of the successive epochs through which the earth passed before man was created. But we omit all those periods, which might perhaps be of interest to the enthusiastic geologist, and come down to the account given of the first meeting of Adam and Eve. Says our author :

There is no God but he ; the Living, the Eternal. Nor slumber seizeth him, nor sleep ; his, whatsoever is in the heavens and whatsoever is in the earth ! Who is he that can intercede with him but by his own permission? He knoweth what hath been before them, and what shall be after them ; yet nought of his knowledge shall they grasp, save what he willeth. His throne reacheth over the heavens and the earth, and the upholding of both burdeneth him not ; and he is the High, the Great. "—*Rodwell's Translation.*

[1] Sura xxiv. 35.   [2] Sura xxiv. 44.

[3] Sura iii. 129.   An item in a list of classes of persons who shall be blessed in this world and go to heaven when they die.

When Adam first met Eve he was walking upon the sea, and he said to her, "Who art thou?" And she said, "I am the destroyer of mercies." And Adam said, "*Who* art thou?" And she said, "I am the destroyer of wealth; he who finds wealth, finds me, and he who does not find wealth does not find me." And Adam said, "*Who* art thou?" And she said, "I am one in whom no faith is to be reposed—*I am Eve.*" And Adam said, "I believe thee, O Eve." And Adam took her, and she conceived and brought forth forty twins, a male and a female at each birth, and all died except Seth, who was the father of Noah, etc.

The author then proceeds to trace the descendants of Noah, assigning to Shem, Ham, and Japheth the countries in which it is commonly understood that they respectively settled.

The next paper is a very elaborate and accurately written manuscript, styled "The Book of Psalms which God sent down to David." We have been puzzled to account for the origin and purpose of this paper. Whatever it comes out of, it is certain it does not come out of the Psalms of David. It contains, however, some excellent moral teachings, written not in Koranic language, but on the whole in very good Arabic, singularly free from those omissions and misplacements of diacritical points which are so troublesome in some Arabic writings. The arrangement of the vowels reveals a thorough acquaintance with the niceties of classical Arabic. It was copied for us from an old manuscript brought by a scribe from Kankan, but he could give no information as to its original source. The statement that it *is* the Psalms is probably a mere freak of the compiler or copyist, unless we suppose the existence of some Mohammedan pseudo-psalmist in the interior. Moreover, the word *anzala* used in the manuscript, which we have translated "*sent down*," is not the word applied in the Koran to David's revelations. The word there used is *âta'*, signifying to *commit*, to *give*, etc. The paper is divided into six chapters or parts. We will give, with the introductory formula and blessing, the first, fourth, and fifth parts.

In the name of God, etc. God bless our lord Mohammed, His prophet, and his family and his wives and his descendants and his friends, and keep them safe.

This is the Book of Psalms which God sent down to David. Peace upon him!

Part the First.

I wonder at him who has heard of Death, how he can rejoice.

I wonder at him who has heard of the Reckoning, how he can gather riches.

I wonder at him who has heard of the Grave, how he can laugh.

I wonder at him who grieves over the waste of his riches and does not grieve over the waste of his life.

I wonder at him who has heard of the future world and its bliss and its enduringness, how he can rest when he has never sought it.

I wonder at him who has heard of the present world and its transitoriness, how he can be secure about it when he has never fled from it.

I wonder at him who is knowing in the tongue and ignorant in the heart.

I wonder at him who is busy with people's faults and forgets his own faults.

I wonder at him who knows that God considers him in all places, how he can rebel against him.

I wonder at him who has purified himself with water and is not pure in his heart.

I wonder at him who knows that he shall die alone, and enter the grave alone, and render account alone, how he can seek reconciliation with men when he has not sought reconciliation with his Lord.

There is no God but God, in truth ; Mohammed is the Envoy of God. God bless him and save him !

PART THE FOURTH.

Son of Man ! Be not of them who are long of repentance and long of hope,[1] and look for the last day without work, and say the say of the servants, and work the work of the hypocrite, and are not satisfied if I give to you, and endure not if I keep from you ; who prescribe that which is approved and good, and do it not, and forbid that which is disapproved and evil, and forego it not, and love the faithful and are not of them, and hate the hypocrites and are of them—exacting and not exact.

Son of Man ! There is not a new day but the earth addresses thee, and thus says she her say unto thee :

Son of Man !

Thou walkest on my back, but thy return is to my belly ;

Thou laughest on my back, and then thou weepest in my belly ;

Thou art joyful on my back, and then thou art sorrowful in my belly ;

Thou sinnest on my back, and then thou sufferest in my belly ;

Thou eatest thy desire on my back, and then the worms eat thee in my belly ;

Son of Man !

I am the house of desolation, I am the house of isolation ;

I am the house of darkness, I am the house of straitness ;

I am the house of question, I am the house of terrors ;

I am the house of serpents, I am the house of scorpions ;

I am the house of thirst, I am the house of hunger ;

[1] That is, waiting on Providence without attempting to " work out one's own salvation."

I am the house of disgrace, I am the house of fires ;
Then cultivate me, and burn [1] me not.

PART THE FIFTH.

Son of Man ! I did not create you to get greatness by you
instead of bitterness, nor to get companionship by you instead
of desolation, nor to borrow by you anything I wanted ; nor
did I create you to draw to me any profit, or to thrust from me
any loss, (far be it from Him the Exalted !) But I have created
you to serve me perpetually, and thank me greatly, and praise
me morning and evening.[2] And if the first of you and the last
of you, and the living of you and the dead of you, and the
small of you and the great of you, and the male of you and the
female of you, and the lords of you and the servants of you,
and the men of you and the beasts of you, if they combine to
obey me, this will not add to my dominion the weight of a
grain of dust. "Whoever does good service, does good service
only for himself ; and whoever is unthankful—why, God is independent of the three worlds." [3]

Son of Man !
As thou lendest, shalt thou borrow ;
As thou workest, shalt thou be recompensed ;
As thou sowest, shalt thou reap.

We have been surprised to notice that the manuscripts which we receive generally from Boporo, Misadu, and Kankan are much better written, and of a
much more edifying character, than those we have
seen from the Sambia and that region of country.
Some of the latter, consisting of childish legends and
superstitious details, are often curious philologically,
being mixtures of Arabic and the vernacular dialect.
It is said also by those who have seen Mohammedan

[1] This is probably a warning against the practice among the
natives of denuding the earth by burning the wood when preparing to plant.

[2] Compare Psalm l. 7–14.   [3] Koran xxix. 5.

worship conducted by the Jalofs and Foulahs about the Sambia and Senegal, and have witnessed similar exercises among the Mandingoes in the region of country east of Liberia, that the latter exhibit in their bearing and proceedings during their religious services greater intelligence, order, and regularity than the former.

During a visit of three weeks made to Boporo in the Mohammedan month of Ramadhan, (December and January, 1868–69.) we had an opportunity of seeing the Mandingo Moslem at home. It being the sacred month of fasting and religious devotedness, we witnessed several religious ceremonies and performances.

As in all Moslem communities, prayer is held five times a day. When the hour for prayer approaches, a man appointed for the purpose, with a very strong and clear voice, goes to the door of the mosque and chants the *adhan*, or call to prayer. This man is called the Mueddin.[1] His call is especially solemn and interesting in the early hours of the morning. We often lay in bed between four and five o'clock listening for the cry of the Mueddin. There was a simple and solemn melody in the chant at that still hour, which after it had ceased still lingered pleasantly on the ear, and often despite ourselves drew us out to the mosque. The morning *adhan*, as we heard it at

[1] The first Moslem crier was an Ethiopian Negro, Bilál by name, "a man of powerful frame and sonorous voice." He was the favorite attendant of Mohammed. Mr. Irving informs us that on the capture of Jerusalem he made the first *adhan*, "at the Caliph Omar's command, and summoned the true believers to prayers with a force of lungs that astonished the Jewish inhabitants."—*Irving's Successors of Mahomet*, p. 100.

Boporo, is as follows: "*Allāhu Akbaru,* (this is said four times.) *Ashhadu anla ilāha ill' Allahu,* (twice). *Ashhadu anna Mohammada rasoolu 'llāhi,* (twice.) *Heiya ala Salāh,* (twice.) *Heiya ala-l-felāh,* (twice.) *Salātu kheiru min a-naumi,* (twice.) *Allāhu Akbaru,* (twice.) *La ilāha ill' Allāhu,* (once.)*[1]* Says Mr. Deutsch:

> Maybe some stray reader remembers a certain thrill on waking suddenly in the middle of his first night on Eastern soil —waking, as it were, from dream into dream. For there came a voice, solitary, sweet, sonorous, floating from on high through the moonlight stillness—the voice of the blind Muëddin, singing the *Ulah,* or first call to prayer. . . . The sounds went and came—*Allāhu, Akbar, Allāhu Akbar*—and this reader may have a vague notion of Arabic and Koranic sound, one he will never forget.[2]

At Boporo and other African towns we have visited this call is made three times within the half hour immediately preceding worship. Before the third call is concluded the people have generally assembled in the mosque. Then the Imám proceeds with the exercises, consisting usually of certain short chapters from the Koran and a few prayers, interspersed with beautiful chanting of the Moslem watch-word, *La ilaha ill' Allāhu, Mohammadu rasoolu 'llahi*—There is no god, etc. We may remark, by the way, that their tunes are not set in the minor key, as is almost always the case among the Arabs. Their natures are more

[1] The English is, "God is most great (four times). I testify that there is no deity but God (twice). I testify that Mohammed is the apostle of God (twice). Come to prayer (twice). Come to security (twice). Prayer is better than sleep (twice). God is most great (twice). There is no deity but God (once)."

[2] "Quarterly Review," October, 1869.

joyful. They exult in the diatonic scale of life, and leave their oriental co-religionists to wail in the sad and mournful chromatics of the desert.

The Mandingoes are an exceedingly polite and hospitable people. The restraints of their religion regulate their manners and control their behavior. Both in speech and demeanor they appear always solicitous to be *en regle*—anxious to maintain the strictest propriety—and they succeed in conforming to the natural laws of etiquette, of which they seem to have an instinctive and agreeable appreciation. In their salutations they always strive to exceed each other in good wishes. The salutation, *Salaam aleikum*—"Peace be with you"—common in oriental Mohammedan countries, is used by them very sparingly, and, as a general thing, only on leaving the mosque after early morning worship. The reply is, *Aleikum-e-Salaam, wa rahmatu 'llahi wa barakatuhu*—"With you be peace, and the mercy of God and his blessing." If *Salaam aleikum* is addressed to them by a Kafir or pagan they seldom reply; if by a Christian, the reply is, *Salaam ala man taba el-huda*—"Peace to him who follows the right way."

Those who speak Arabic speak the Koranic or book Arabic, preserving the final vowels of the classical language—a practice which, in the hurry and exigencies of business life, has been long discontinued in countries where the language is vernacular; so that in Egypt and Syria the current speech is very defective, and clipped and corrupted. Mr. Palgrave informs us, however, that in North-east Arabia the "grammatical dialect" is used in ordinary conversation. "The

smallest and raggedest child that toddles about the
street lisps in the correctest book Arabic that ever De
Sacy studied or Sibaweeyah professed ."[1] So among
the Arabic scholars whom one meets in the interior
of Liberia. In proper names we hear Ibraheem*a*,
Alee*u*, Suleiman*a*, Abdullah*i*, Daud*a*, etc.; in worship
Allah*u*, Akbar*u*, Lailah*a*, ill'Allah*u*, etc.; and it is
difficult for the mere tyro in Arabic pronunciation
either to understand or make himself understood unless
he constantly bear in mind the final vowels in nouns,
verbs, and adjectives. A recent number of the
" Saturday Review," [2] in a notice of General Daumas's
new work on "Arabic Life and Mussulman Society,"
remarks, " One comfort for the learner will be that the
oft-pressed distinction between what is termed the
learned and the vulgar (Arabic) tongue is a mere
fiction of European growth. It has no foundation in
native usage." We fear that the theoretical comfort
which the soothing reviewer attempts to administer to
the learner of Arabic will be found of no practical avail
when applied to the intercourse of daily life in Syria
and Egypt. Only such learned natives as Mr. Bistany
of Beyroot and Dr. Meshakah of Damascus speak the
language so as to be understood by one versed only in
Koranic inflections. And even they generally avoid
that style as stilted, pedantic, and absurd. Says a
higher authority : [3]

Les populations Arabes, en général, etant fort ignorantes,
par leur misère d'abord, et ensuite par l'extreme difficulté de

[1] Palgrave's Arabia, vol. i. p. 311.   [2] March 26, 1870.
[3] M. Bresnier, Professor of Arabic in the Normal College of Al-
giers, in his " *Cours Pratique et Theorique de Langue Arabe.*"

l'etude et de l'application de leur idiome, le langage usuel des diverses regions est soumis à bien des varietés, soit de prononciation, soit de *denomination* des ideés et des choses.

Among the Moslems of West Africa there are some peculiarities in the sounds of the letters. The fourth letter of the alphabet is generally pronounced like *s ;* the seventh like the simple *k ;* the ninth like *j* in jug ; *seen* and *sheen* have both the sound of *s.* The fifteenth letter is sounded like *l ;* the nineteenth, whose guttural sound is so difficult to Western organs, is sounded like *k ;* the twenty-first like *g* hard.

The introduction of Islam into Central and West Africa has been the most important if not the sole preservative against the desolations of the slave-trade. Mohammedanism furnished a protection to the tribes who embraced it by effectually binding them together in one strong religious fraternity, and enabling them by their united effort to baffle the attempts of powerful pagan slave hunters. Enjoying this comparative immunity from sudden hostile incursions, industry was stimulated among them ; industry diminished their poverty, and as they increased in worldly substance, they also increased in desire for knowledge. Gross superstition gradually disappeared from among them. Receiving a degree of culture from the study of the Arabic language, they acquired loftier views, wider tastes, and those energetic habits which so pleasingly distinguish them from their pagan neighbors.

Large towns and cities have grown up under Mohammedan energy and industry. Dr. Barth was surprised to find such towns or cities as Kanó and Sokoto in the centre of Africa—to discover the focus

of a complex and widely ramified commerce, and a
busy hive of manufacturing industry, in a region which
most people had believed to be a desert. And there
are towns and cities nearly as important farther west,
to which Barth did not penetrate, affording still scope
to extend the horizon of European knowledge and the
limits of commercial enterprise. Mr. Benjamin Anderson, the enterprising Liberian traveller, who has
recently visited Misodu, the capital of the Western
Mandingoes, about two hundred miles east of Monrovia, describes that city as the centre of a considerable
commerce, reaching as far north as Senegal and east
as far as Sokoto.

The African Moslems are also great travellers.
They seem to travel through the country with greater
freedom and safety than any other people, on account,
probably, of their superior intelligence and greater
usefulness. They are continually crossing the continent to Egypt, Arabia, and Syria. We met a few
weeks ago at Toto-coreh, a town about ten miles east
of Boporo, a lad who informed us that he was born at
Mecca while his parents were in that city on pilgrimage.
We gave him a copy of the New Testament in Arabic,
which he read with unimpeded fluency, and with the
Oriental accent and pronunciation.

The general diffusion of the Arabic language [1] in

---

[1] The natives love and revere the language. All documents of a
serious character must be written in that language. Bishop Crowther of the Niger, in a letter dated October 30, 1869, tells us of his
visit to King Masaba, a distinguished Mohammedan sovereign, with
whom he entered into a written agreement with reference to the
establishment of a Christian mission in his capital. "I drew up his
promise," says the Bishop, "in English, which he handed over to

this country through Mohammedan influence must be regarded as a preparatory circumstance of vast importance for the introduction of the Gospel. It may be "the plan of Providence that these many barbarous nations of Africa are to be consolidated under one aggressive empire of ideas and faith, to prepare the way for evangelization through the medium of one copious, cultivated, expressive tongue, in the place of leaving to the Church the difficult task of translating and preaching in many barbarous languages, incapable of expressing the finer forms of thought."[1] Already some of the vernaculars have been enriched by expressions from the Arabic for the embodiment of the higher processes of thought. They have received terms regarding the religion of the one God, and respecting a certain state of civilization, such as marrying, reading, writing, and the objects having relation thereto, sections of time, and phrases of salutation and of good breeding; then the terms relating to dress, instruments, and the art of warfare, as well as architecture, commerce, etc.[2]

Mohammedanism in this part of the world could easily be displaced by Christian influence if Christian organizations would enter with vigor into this field. Rev. G. W. Gibson, Rector of Trinity Church, Monrovia, in a letter published in the "Spirit of Missions" for April, 1869, says :

his Maalims *to be translated into Arabic."—Christian Observer*, January, 1870.

[1] Prof. Post, of Syrian Prot. College, Beyroot.

[2] See Barth's "Collection of Central African Vocabularies," Part I. p. 29.

5

Whatever may have been the influence of Mohammedanism on races in other parts of the world, I think here, upon the African, results will prove it to be merely preparatory to a Christian civilization. In this country, and almost immediately in our vicinity, it has recovered millions from paganism, without, I think, having such a grasp upon the minds of the masses as to lead them obstinately to cling to it in preference to Christianity, with its superior advantages. The same feelings which led them to abandon their former religion for the Moslem will, no doubt, lead them still further, and induce them to embrace ours when properly presented. I express this opinion the more readily from several interviews I have had lately with prominent parties connected with some of these tribes.

We are persuaded that with the book knowledge they already possess, and their love of letters, many of them would become ready converts of a religion which brings with it the recommendation of a higher culture and a nobler civilization. And, once brought within the pale of Christianity, these Mohammedans would be a most effective agency for the propagation of the Gospel in remote regions, hitherto impervious to European zeal and enterprise, and the work of African regeneration would proceed with uninterrupted course and unexampled rapidity.

IX.
REMARKABLE CONDITION OF THE AFRI-CAN FIELD.

[The following Extracts are from a recent paper issued by the Board of Missions of the Protestant Episcopal Church.]

SPREAD out before the Church is a country of con-siderable elevation, comparative salubrity, and ex-ceeding beauty, diversified with hills and valleys, rich in its mineral and agricultural products, irrigated, says one traveller, by beautiful streams of water which would apparently give life to the dead by their exhilarating coolness and purity.

The tribes of this interior region are larger than those upon the coast, and exercise their power and influence over corresponding areas of country, an im-portant fact in view of Missionary enterprise. They are free to a degree from the petty jealousies and rivalries which characterize the smaller tribes border-ing the Atlantic and prevent free travel and extended intercourse.

Its inhabitants are people of manly presence, full of enterprise and intelligence, bent on bettering their condition and ready to receive improvement from any source, from Mohammedanism on the East, or from Christianity on the West.

And now, to the shame of the Christian Church, there is a probability that the Crescent and not the Cross, will be planted upon the coast of Western Africa.

"The yearning of the native African," says Rev Mr. Crummell, "for a higher religion, is illustrated by the singular fact, that Mohammedanism is rapidly and *peaceably* spreading all through the tribes of Western Africa, even to the Christian settlements of Liberia." "From Senegal to Lagos, over two thousand miles," says Professor Blyden, "there is scarcely an important settlement on the sea-board, where there are not at least one mosque and active representatives of Islam, often side by side with the Christian teacher."

The opinion which prevails that the Missionary work in behalf of the heathen in Africa may be left to the Liberians, is a fatal mistake. They are a poor people, and it is with difficulty that they can support the institutions of religion among themselves; and the history of Missions in Liberia shows that whenever Christians in this country have ceased to send out white Missionaries, the work among the heathen has come to nothing.

AN ACCOUNT OF THE NEW FIELD.

Near the northern end of Liberia there juts out into the sea a bold promontory, 1500 feet high, known as Cape Mount. Bishop Payne, in his report to the Board of Missions, at its session in October, 1870, wrote: "A Mission establishment on the top of this mountain would have all the advantages of elevation

that Bohlen Station has, eighty miles interior, with the
further very great blessing of a constant fresh sea-
breeze."

There is a highway to the interior from the neighborhood of Cape Mount. Whatever facts have been
gleaned regarding the interior tribes, will therefore be
presented to the reader, beginning at Cape Mount and
taking the tribes in order as a traveller would come
upon them passing interiorward; though it is probable that two of the most important tribes, the Pessas
and the Barlines, can be reached with greatest facility,
not by way of Cape Mount, but from the St. John's
River.

The country immediately around Cape Mount is
inhabited by

THE VYE (OR VEY) TRIBE.

" They are the most intelligent," says Bishop Payne,
" of any on the West Coast. It was this people who,
some fifteen years ago, invented a syllabic alphabet.
They hold constant intercourse with the Mandingoes
and other Mohammedan tribes far in the interior.
And these intelligent neighbors are fast converting
them to their false faith."

The language of the Veys (or Vyes) serves as a
medium of communication between a number of the
tribes interior.

THE CONDOES—NEXT INTERIORWARD.

Their king, Marmoru, exerts great influence over all
the neighboring tribes, and is thus reported of by an
English traveller and writer, W. Winwood Reade, Esq.

Copy of a written statement made by Mr. W. Win-

wood Reade, and left with Marmoru, King of the
Condo country :

Тото-Korie, Jan. 22, 1870.

I desire to state that having paid a visit to Marmoru, King
of Boporo, resident in this town, he received me hospitably,
and made me a handsome present when I left him.

Marmoru is evidently the most powerful king in the regions
interior of Monrovia. He possesses the road from Musardu
and other inland states to the sea ; the whole of their trade is
therefore in his hands.

It is my opinion that the favor of this king should be cultivated, not only by the Liberian Government, but also by Missionaries, travellers, and foreign merchants.

Marmoru having received some education in Liberia, has
much larger views than most native chiefs. On the present
occasion, a school having been established under the auspices
of Professor Blyden, of Liberia College, he has shown a most
laudable desire to further the education of the children of
his town ; he is also desirous that Missionaries, and indeed
settlers generally, should take up their abode with him.

Toto-Korie, situated about ten miles east of Boporo, appears
to me to be well adapted for a settlement ; as a trading station,
it offers remarkable advantages, receiving as it does all the produce from the interior ; the soil is suitable for all the require-
ments of a plantation ; the situation seems healthy ; stores,
etc., can be brought up from the settlements in three days ;
and it is naturally of advantage to those who attempt to exercise a moral and educational influence over these people, that
their ruler should be well disposed towards projects of that
kind, and apparently so well acquainted with the value of
knowledge.

(Signed)   W. Winwood Reade.

The school to which Mr. Reade refers is that established by our Missionary, Rev. Mr. Gibson, and
taught by a catechist under his charge. It is as yet

an inconsiderable enterprise. GOD grant it may prove to be the beginning by our Church of a hearty, resolute, large-minded effort to do her duty. The circumstances of the establishment of this school are thus described by Professor Blyden of the College in Liberia, and by the Rev. Mr. Gibson ·

MONROVIA, *Feb.* 5, 1870.

I have just returned from a brief visit to the Boporo regions. Mr. W. Winwood Reade, an English traveller, author of *Savage Africa*, accompanied me. Rev. G. W. Gibson, of the Episcopal Church, anxious to respond to the urgent calls which are so loudly made for teachers from that quarter, sent out with me one of his candidates for orders, to open a school in that country. The King, Marmoru, was not at Boporo when we reached that town, but at Toto-Korie, a fortified town ten miles on the east. We proceeded thither, where the king received us in fine style, and especially welcomed the teacher. Two days after we arrived, on Friday, January 21st, he called his principal men together in a large open building in the town, and presented in their presence his own and his brother's children, to form the nucleus of a school.

He exhorted the people on the importance of such establishments among them. He said that he himself having lived a little while at Monrovia when a boy—sent thither by King Boatswain, his father—had gained some insight into civilization, which had proved of much advantage to him ; and he only regretted that his knowledge was so exceedingly limited. He now felt grateful for the opportunity afforded him of introducing among the children of the country the advantage of book-learning.

I then read a chapter from the Bible, and prayed, after which I took down the names of the boys presented, and gave them primers. They seemed delighted. After introducing to them the teacher—who made a few remarks—and entreating them to be kind to him, I dismissed the assembly by permission of the king. That was a day long to be remembered by all who were present. To me it was a great and solemn privilege. Mr. Winwood Reade, who proclaims himself a freethinker, and who has not much faith in Missions as religious agencies, could not resist the influence of the occasion. He drew up a paper giving his impressions of the country, etc., which he left with the king. I send you a copy herewith.

Mr. Gibson has assumed a great responsibility in opening a school at Toto-Korie. I hope he will be sustained by his Board. The Episcopalians are thus first in the field ; but the field is large and needy.

Under date of February 2d, 1870, the Rev. M. Gibson wrote regarding this enterprise :

Here, then, we have a most flourishing school and station, in the centre of this interesting region of country, at the rich metropolis and capital towns of Boporo and Toto-Korie, where not less than ten different tribes are largely represented. There that school may have the patronage and protection of a powerful king, ruling over not less, it is supposed, than forty or fifty thousand inhabitants. . . . .
A dry, healthy atmosphere, rich country, abounding in beautiful landscapes, elevated hills, rich valleys, with charming streams of water murmuring along, present an inviting aspect. Here, horses thrive, and cattle abound, while the eyes may feast upon the extensive rice and cotton fields, from the latter of which are annually manufactured those immense quantities of cloths that find their way to the Liberia, Sierra Leone, and other markets. Here rich markets are open, supplied from a vast area of country. But here, too, is the Mohammedan mosque, and the pagan shrine. Alas !

" Every prospect pleases, and only man is vile."

August 19th, 1870, he wrote :

I received intelligence from our Toto-Korie station three days ago. The little school seems to be doing well ; several of the pupils are reading books—others spelling. Mr. Tucker (the Catechist) is pleased with the field and hopes to be useful to the people.

REPORT OF A LIBERIAN EXPLORER.

The Liberian Government, in 1868, sent out an exploring expedition to the interior country. We give such extracts from the journal of Mr. Anderson, the explorer, as tend to throw light upon the country and the people.

Of Boporo, the capital of the Condo tribe, he says : Boporo is in latitude 7 deg. 45 min. 8 sec. Its elevation above the level of the sea is about 560 feet. The barometer, in the months of May and June, stands from 29. 18 to 29. 40 ; the thermometer ranges from 78 to 80 Fahrenheit. It is situated on .a small plain near the foot of some high hills E. N. E. of it. Very high hills rise on every side, with an elevation from 300 to 650 feet, coursing along in every direction, some continuing three or four miles in length before their spurs come down into the valleys or plains.

The population of Boporo is of a mixed character, such as war, commerce, and the domestic slave-trade are calculated to produce ; in consequence of which there are as many different languages spoken as there are tribes ; Vey, Golah, Mambomah, Mandingo, Pessy, Boondee, Boozie, and Hurrah languages. The Vey language is used for general communication. The extent and population of these tribes are very variable elements. The population living in the towns may be set down at 3,000, but then there are many outlying

5*

villages and hamlets; and considering these as the
suburbs of Boporo, they undoubtedly raise the
population to 10,000.

The Mandingoes possess strong moral influence.
Scarcely anything is undertaken without consulting
their priests, whose prayers, blessings, and other rites
are supposed to give a propitious turn to all the affairs
of peace and war. They are Mohammedans; but as
the ruder tribes do not addict themselves to the
intellectual habits of the Mandingoes, it has been
found necessary to adjust that faith to the necessities
of the case; and to temper some of the mummeries of
fetichism with the teachings of Islam. Yet are there
to be found individuals who do not prostitute their
faith, and who are more scrupulous and sincere. It is
believed by many persons that the Arabic learning of
our Mandingoes, in reading and writing from the
Koran, is merely mechanical, or a mere matter of
memory; but Kaifal took a small Arabic grammar
given me by Professor Blyden, and showed himself
thoroughly versed in all the distinctions of person,
gender, number, etc., in the conjugation of a verb.
However, all are not equally proficient in this respect.

They have a mosque at Boporo, where nothing
enjoined by their religion is omitted. It is attended
solely by the Mandingoes, none of the other tribes
visiting it; not because they are prohibited, for the
Mandingoes would make proselytes of them all if
they could. It is sufficient for the "Kaffirs," (unbelievers,) as they are denominated by the Mandingoes, to buy the amulets, necklaces, and belts containing transcripts from the Koran sewed up in them,

to be worn around the neck, arms or waist as preservatives from the casualties of war, sickness, or ill-luck in trade or love.

The Mandingoes are scrupulously attentive to their worship. They regularly attend their services three times a day : five o'clock in the morning ; three o'clock in the afternoon ; and seven o'clock in the evening.

In these services I was particularly attracted by the manner in which they chanted the cardinal article of their creed ; and many a morning have I been reminded of my own duty, by their solemn musical voices reciting :

La il - la - ha il - al - la - hu Ma-hamma-du ra-sul il - la - hi.[1]

Boporo has a small market, held in the north-east suburbs of the town. The bartering is carried on solely by women. There is no established currency ; the exchange takes place of one commodity for another, according to their mutual necessities. It is generally attended by one hundred and seventy-five to two hundred persons. The articles are palm-oil, rice, kaffee-seed, shallots—a small species of onion— meat, cotton stripes, tobacco, kola, earthen pots, etc. A great many country cloths are made at Boporo, every family having a small loom. They would economize both time and labor if they would employ our large loom, instead of the narrow six-inch loom they use. I have no doubt they would do so, if any civilized person would interest himself to show them.

. " There is no Deity but God. Mohammed is the Apostle of God."

These people are very sensible of the superiority of everything that comes from (Dru-kau) Monrovia, and they attempt to practice our civilization of themselves. The king has a frame house at Totoquella, with a piazza surrounding it, all of native construction. He also uses chairs, tables, beds, bedsteads, looking-glasses, scented soaps, colognes, etc. He took great interest in examining my sextant, and even the pictures in my books; but that which afforded him the greatest pleasure was the stereoscope. He entreated me so earnestly to leave it with him, that I felt myself bound to gratify his wishes in that respect, though I had specially intended it for Musardu.

He was no less satisfied when I flattered him with the prospect of a school for children being established at Boporo, telling me that when John B. Jordan traded there, he was accustomed to get Jordan to teach him. The king spells a little, and is somewhat acquainted with numbers. This is the place for the Missionary to be of service; but it seems that, though Mohammed has a small mosque and school at Vannswah, almost in the Virginia settlement, the Christians have neither church nor school at Boporo.

Adjoining the Condoes on the east is the

PESSA TRIBE.

Their country is three days from Monrovia, northeast, say seventy-five miles. They were visited some ten or fifteen years ago by Mr. George B. Seymour, a most intelligent Liberian colonist, an emigrant from Hartford, Connecticut. While engaged in lucrative business near the coast, he was so moved by the spiritual destitution and misery of the heathen tribes that he relinquished his business and went and settled among the Pessas.

He started from Bexley, on the St. John's River, near the coast, and planted himself at a point about one hundred miles interior. He made most pathetic appeals to the Christians of this country that they would occupy for CHRIST the field which he had opened, but in vain ; and on his death the effort came to nought. From his journal the following extracts are made :

"The Cam Wood (Dye Stuff), Palm Oil, and Ivory Districts begin in the Pessa country, and extend into the Barline country. . . . . . . The people make their clothes, iron, tobacco, pipes, bowls, basins, pots, bread, meat, oil, salt, and everything necessary for sustenance. . . . . . . They are kind and industrious, hospitable to strangers, but like all savages, revengeful to their enemies. At the same time they are disposed to tricks of dishonesty, and will take advantage of strangers if they can.

One thing I have observed favorable to the spread of the Gospel is, that the tribe are not given up to the use of the gree-gree, like the Bassas. . . . . . . Their aptness to learn is much in advance of the Bassas, and their dialect is peculiarly adapted to the articulation of English, and they speak it with a clearness that would deceive many an ear. The country is of a rolling and mountainous character. The climate is cool and salubrious, and considerably behind the season at Bassa, say six or eight weeks. The rainy season is not so heavy by one-third, as

on the coast.   The thermometer stands on an average
at 87 deg. at Bassa all the year ; here I am sure much
lower, for the same kind of clothing as is in use in
New England, is very acceptable at this place a good
part of the year. . . . . . . It is my opinion
that a company of emigrants this distance out, would
experience little inconvenience from fever, if prudent.
As to the country beyond us, we can travel to
any distance in safety, as far as we have learned from
our people, and they are acquainted with three other
tribes interior.   The native hails with joy the ap-
proach of a stranger to his country. . . . . These
people are very inquisitive, and seem apt to catch an
idea of anything new as soon as it is presented
to them.   They can be made, by prayerful labor
a good and great people.   They possess no little
sense of home and country.   They seem very desirous
of cultivating a friendly familiarity with all persons.
They all expressed, with the greatest warmth, desire
for education for the children and youth among
them—in fact this was the general desire wherever
we travelled."   The Liberian Professor, E. W. Blyden,
writes :

"Here is a field entirely open to the Gospel.   Is
there no society in America willing to enter it ?   . .
I suppose there is no portion of Africa where the
people in a purely heathen condition are so . accessible, and there is no part of the world where civilized
settlers would have less trouble."   When Seymour
visited them, in 1857, the headmen sent the following
petition, and they have made a similar request, in
vain, every year since then :

CAMWOOD FOREST, PESSA COUNTRY, *Aug.* 13, 1857.

DEAR SIR : Hearing of your kind wishes and desires for our much-injured country, and your expectation to send some good American amongst us, we felt it but our duty to say that we shall hail the event with gladness.   .   .   . We, your humble servants, are willing to do all we can to aid in the matter. We are willing to give a tract of land for a settlement. We want Americans among us to teach us the letters, and above all, the Christian religion.

Signed by three Kings and Headmen.

Beyond the Pessa lies the

BARLINE COUNTRY,

Regarding which a late explorer, Mr. Spencer Anderson, gives the following facts, in addition to those which are given in the letter from the Rev. Mr. Crummell. Mr. Anderson started from the coast. His route lay through the Queah and Pessa countries. Eight days' journey, on foot, from Careysburg, brought him to Palaka, the capital of Barlines. He found the tribe friendly and hospitable, and anxious for relations with the Government of Liberia. The king was so pleased that he entrusted his son to Mr. Anderson, to be brought up in civilization and Christianity.

He reports that the Cam-wood Forest begins in the Pessa country, six days' walk from Careysburg, north-east by east, and extends, with slight intervals, to a great distance beyond Palaka, and that the climate is much drier and freer from miasmatic influences than on the coast.

The land of the Barlines has been thrown open to

Missionary effort in a most remarkable way, as the following communication from the Rev. Mr. Crummell shows:

I write to inform you of a recent opening for Missions, which seems to me more important and promising than any other we have ever had, and which, I judge, you will decide ought to be seized upon without delay.

At the distance of about one hundred and twenty miles interiorward, is the country of the Barline people ; a lofty, cool, mountainous country, containing a large and crowded population, numerous towns, unusual and superior civil regulations, and distinguished, withal, by great industrial energies. The capital of the country is a large city, surrounded by a wall of stone ; here two market days are kept every week, and thousands of people, even from remote distances, come with both domestic and foreign goods, provisions, and cattle in large numbers for sale. Important manufactures are carried on in all this region. The people make all their own warlike and agricultural instruments : cultivate and cure their own tobacco ; weave their own cloth ; prepare their own salt.

But they are heathen and cannibals, and are imbruted by all the grossness and ferocity of deadly superstition. Indeed, the section in which they live is a part of that vast interior land which I believe to be the darkest place on earth : that quarter of the continent where never Missionary or traveller has penetrated for adventure, or for the purpose of carrying the 'glad tidings.' Two hundred miles from the coast there is a vast range of country, extending from about longitude 3 deg. to longitude 10 deg. west of Greenwich ; which, without doubt, has remained for ages isolate and disconnected from the outer world ; where Christian or Mohammedan never trod ; and where, save by a few visits from the Cavalla Missionaries, and especially by my former pupil, Rev. Mr. Seton, heathenism has revelled for ages, undisturbed in its own rank and deadly barbarities.

The government of Liberia has recently sent a Commissioner to the kings and headmen of this country. He was received with gladness and distinction. With the utmost willingness they ceded their territory to the Liberian government, and our national flag now floats within the bounds of their capital. The chief motive which has led them so cordially to subject themselves to Liberian authority is the desire for an easy access to the coast, and safety and security in journeys thereto. The faith of the Liberian government is pledged to them, that this security and safety shall be fully given to them. Already, block-houses, small forts, are being erected at stages of fifteen and twenty miles, for the purpose of keeping open roads, and maintaining peace on the road to this country. . . . The chiefs and headmen express strong desires for teachers, for the instruction of their children ; and declare their willingness to receive Missionaries. I have had a long conversation with the Commissioner ; and he assures me that there is now every facility offered for founding a mission among this people. He intends, please God, to make another visit to Barline early in October, in order to convey the chiefs to Monrovia, at the time of the next session of the Legislature in December, and he very kindly gave me the privilege to join his party for a Missionary visit.

I repeat that it is my conviction that this is the greatest, most promising, most secure opening which our Mission has ever had to the interior of Africa. It seems to me desirable that a Missionary should be sent there, *i. e.*, to the capital, without delay ; that a good substantial house should be at once erected ; that a schoolmaster should accompany the Missionary ; that two mature and intelligent and pious females, Liberian women, should be connected with the party ; that a superior outfit should be furnished, so that the Mission should be commenced in the sight of the heathen with strength, and not with a show of weakness and littleness ; with some of the outward seeming that GOD'S Church comes there to do GOD's work in earnestness.

East of the Condo and north of the Barline country, adjacent to both, is the country of

THE DOMAR BONSIES.

Mr. B. Anderson writes: "You no sooner arrive in the Bonsie country, than a contrast of cleanliness, order, and industry strikes you. That tribe, continually represented to us as savage, fierce, and intractable, at once invites you into its large walled towns with all the hospitalities and courtesy that the minds of this simple, untutored people can think of.

"I arrived at Zolu's town on the 8th of July, 1868, at four o'clock, P.M. The walls of this town are from eighteen to twenty feet high, consisting of clay, and very thick. A regular salvo of musketry announced my entrance, and quickly a band of music made its appearance, consisting of twelve large and small ivory horns, and a half dozen drums of various sizes and sounds. I was conducted to the market space, in the centre of the town, and there welcomed amidst the blast and flourish of Bonsie music and the firing of muskets.

"They were astonished and overjoyed that a (Weegee) an American should come so far to visit them in their own country. A thousand strange faces, whom I had never before seen, were gazing at me. After their curiosity and wonder had been satisfied, they gave me spacious and comfortable lodgings, and commenced a series of hospitalities which, from mere quantity alone, became oppressive. . . . . .

"The two great farming staples in the Bonsie country are rice and cotton. Sometimes the rice and cotton are planted together, but most of the cotton-farms succeed the rice-farms, yet they are very large;

for they have to clothe a country densely populated,
where men, women, and children all go clothed, and
no foreign manufactures, scarcely, reach them. Cot-
ton-gins would be a blessing to these people ; for the
manner in which they are obliged to prepare cotton
for spinning is painful and tedious to the last degree
of labor. This part of the labor is done by the women ; the men do the weaving. The spindle is in the
hands of every woman, from the princess to the slave.
The dyeing of cloth is also done by the women, at
which the Mandingoes are the most expert ; and they
know how to impart various shades of blue in a
permanent and beautiful manner. Though they have
abundance of camwood, I have never seen them use
it for the purpose of dyeing. The chief colors used
are blue and yellow ; the latter is extracted from bark.
Taking into account that these people not only clothe
themselves, but furnish the vast number of cloths that
are brought to the coast to be used in the leeward
trade, it shows what the cotton-producing power of
the country would become if this primitive, barbarian
industry were only assisted by some labor-saving
machinery.

"The Bonsie people have very tractable disposi-
tions, and are wedded to no particular species of error.
Fetichism has no strong hold on them. They believe
in that thing most that manifests the greatest visible
superiority or power. They are greatly duped by
the fraud and chicanery of the Mohammedan Mandingo priests.

"In general physical appearance, the Bonzies are
well built, generally from five and a-half to six feet

in stature, with stoutly developed bodies, of sufficient muscular strength to hold a United States musket, bayonet fixed, at full arm's length in one hand. They are an exceedingly healthy people, and of very clean habits. They bathe regularly twice a day, night and morning, in warm water, besides the intermediate cold water baths they are sure to take at whatever creek they happen to cross in their daily walking. For cleaning the teeth, they use a brush made of ratan, admirably adapted to the purpose.'

Next are the

WYMAR BONSIES.

Dowilnyah is the king of the Wymar Bonsies. His messengers were tall black men, with red and restless eyes, tattooed faces, filed teeth, huge spears, and six feet bows. They also had a reputation which remarkably corresponded with their appearance.

The Bonsie country is densely populated. The difference between the Domar and Wymar Bonsie is, that the latter marks his face from his temple to his chin with an indelible blue stain, while the former does not practice tattooing of any kind. This tribe extends from the southwest portion of the Pessy country to the western border of the Mandingo country.

The women are really the industrious part of the population; for while their lords are wholly devoted to pleasure, palavers, and wars, the women are engaged in numerous domestic duties, and especially in spinning cotton. Here, also, as in the Domar country, the spindle is in the hands of every woman, from the princess to the slave. The women, however, enjoy themselves, particularly on market-days, which at this town takes place every Sunday.

This market is seated on the banks of the St. Paul's River, and is carried on under the shade of large cotton (bombax) and acacia trees. The commodities of exchange are country cloths, cotton stripes, raw cotton, iron, soap, palm-oil, palm-butter, ground-nuts, rice, plaintains, bananas, dried fish, dried meat, peas, beans, sweet potatoes, onions (chalots), snuff, tobacco, pipes, salt, earthen pots or vessels for holding water and for cooking purposes, large quantities of Kola slaves, and bullocks. The bullocks are generally brought by the Mandingoes to the market. Palm-wine is not allowed to be sold in the market. Peace and order are secured by persons especially appointed for that purpose. After everybody has assembled on the ground, these preservers of the peace, with long staves in their hands, go through the market, ordering everybody to sit down ; they then admonish the people to carry on their bargains peacefully and without contention. This preliminary being gone through with, the market is opened. It is generally attended by six or seven thousand people. There are several large markets held in the Wymar country; the one at Comma's town is larger than this. The daily market held in the central town is very convenient for making small purchases."

Describing a visit which he made to Ballatah, one of the Boozie towns, Anderson writes : "Ballatah is like the other Boozie towns, but far better laid out. The houses are not crammed so closely together. It contains about twenty-five hundred people ; it is seat-

THE PEOPLE OF AFRICA.

ed in a plain, and is commanded by very high and
abrupt hills on its western side, while the land rolls
off in gentle undulations toward the east. We were
carried to some outlying villages north-west of Ballatah, situated at the foot of the same high hills that
overlook that town. Here they were busy smelting
iron. The furnaces were built of clay, and of a conical shape, from five and a half to six feet high, having
clay pipes or vents close to the bottom, arranged in
groups of two and three, for the purpose of draught.
The charcoal and iron ore are put in at the top. At
the bottom is an opening through which the slag and
other impurities are withdrawn.

"Thursday, December 3d, 1868, we started from
Ballatah. The direction was N.E., and parallel to a
range of very high hills, called the Vukkah hills.
These hills are from seven hundred to one thousand
feet high, and are variously composed of granite, iron
ore, and a reddish clay, which, from the steep slopes
near the top, had shelved down in many places.

"Friday, 4th of December, 1868, we rested at Vukkah. This town stands at the foot of a range of high
hills of the same name. It is the last Boozie town,
and the nearest to the Mandingo country. These
hills, called 'Vukkah' by the Boozies, and 'Fomah'
by the Mandingoes, take a definite direction N.E.
They are the highest range, and form a marked and
acknowledged boundary between the Boozie and
Mandingo territories. At the foot of this range are
seated a number of towns, Boozie and Mandingo."

THE MANDINGOES.

The Mandingoes are an Arabic-speaking Moham-

BALLATAH, A TOWN IN W. AFRICA. ELEPHANTS INVADE ITS COTTON-FIELDS.

medan tribe, and notable traders, who travel over most of the country between their land and the sea, and exert a strong influence over all the other tribes.

They have made considerable advance in education. Mr. Anderson mentions the fact that a Mandingo priest, with whom he was brought in contact, took an Arabic grammar which Mr. Anderson had with him, and showed himself thoroughly versed in all the distinctions of person, gender, number, etc., in the conjugation of a verb.

These people, though Mohammedans, deserve our highest respect. They have cordially and honestly embraced the highest form of religion which was within their reach. Professor Blyden bears witness that the progress of Islam among them presents "the same instances of real and eager mental conflict, of minds in honest transition, of careful comparison and reflection that have been formed in other communities where new aspects of truth and fresh considerations have been placed before them. . . . The Koran is almost always in their hands. It seems to be their labor and their relaxation to pore over its pages. They love to read and recite it for hours together. . . . They are an exceedingly polite and hospitable people. The restraints of their religion regulate their manners and control their behavior. Both in speech and demeanor they appear always solicitous to be *en regle*, and they succeed in conforming to the natural laws of etiquette, of which they seem to have an instinctive and agreeable appreciation. . . . . "Receiving a degree of culture from the study of the Arabic language, they acquired loftier views, wider tastes, and those energetic habits which so pleasingly distinguish them from their pagan neighbors."

These Mandingoes were one of the tribes visited by Anderson. He writes:

"At three o'clock, P. M., we were met on the road by several Mandingoes, who accompanied us to their town, Nu-Somadu, or Mohammadu. The walls of this town are quadrilateral in shape, each side being a series of bastions, which at a distance looks like some old fortified front. The walls, however, are so thin that a four-pounder could demolish them in a very little time.

"We entered the town, and were entertained in a very hospitable manner. A house was given to us, small indeed in its dimensions to what we had been accustomed to in the Boozie country, but convenient and comfortable. Being wearied with the journey, I threw myself into a hammock, and commenced surveying alterations and arrangements which a change in the character of the country had introduced. The house was a circular structure of clay, with a conical roof made entirely of large canebrake and long grass. In looking around the walls, our eyes rested on a saddle, stirrups, bridle, with leather leggings, and a tremendous tower gun.

"Sunday, the 6th of December, we attempted to pursue our journey; but the chief refused to allow us to depart before he had demonstrated his good-will and hospitality. He killed a heifer, and cooked it with onions. We satisfied our appetites, and made him an appropriate present. We then departed, and arrived at Naalah late in the afternoon. In the

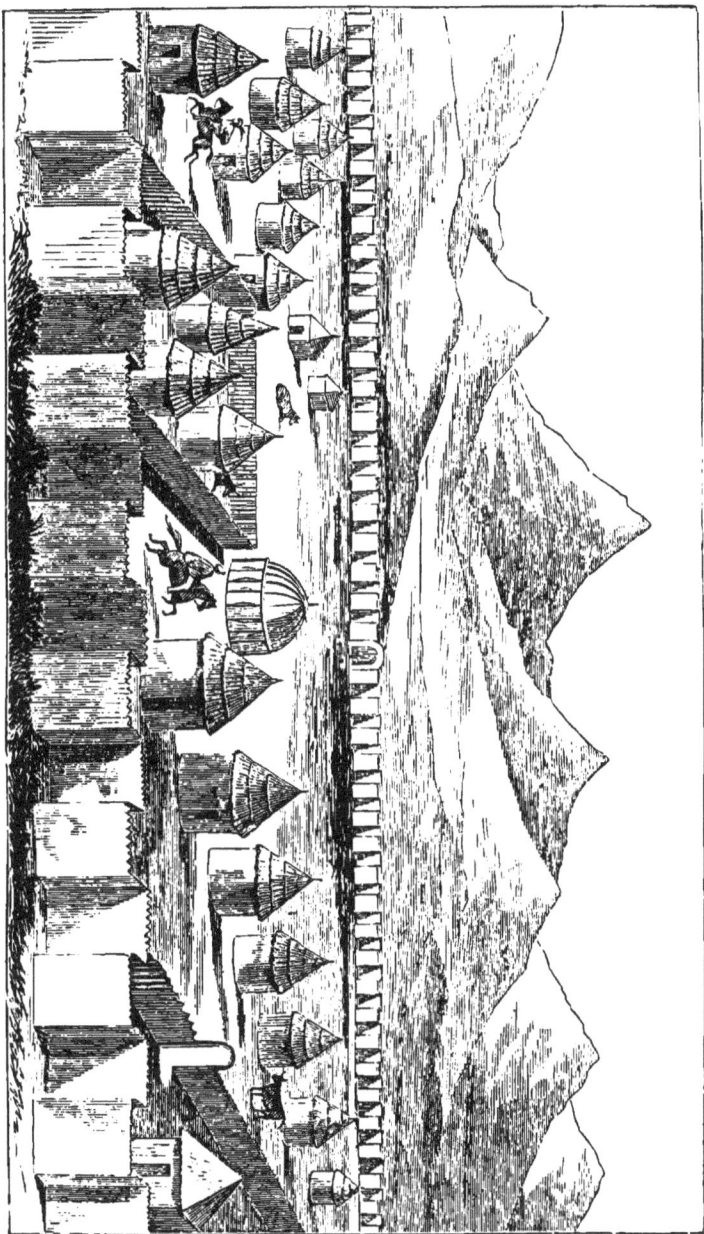

MAHOMMADU—A MANDINGO TOWN, W. AFRICA.

morning, a trooper was at once dispatched to Musardu, to inform them that the Tibbabue (American) had come. In two hours he returned, telling me that the Musardu people requested that I would remain at Naalah until they had made preparations for my reception. I immediately sent them word that I had been so long coming to see their country that I would rather forego any public demonstration than be delayed any further. I was then answered to come on; they would gladly receive me.

"Accompanied by several Mandingoes from Naalah and Mohammadu, we started for Musardu. Our interest in the journey was enlivened by the novel features of the country. In passing through the Boozie country, extensive views were frequently obstructed by a dense vegetation that hemmed in the sight on each side of a narrow foot-path. Here the peculiar features of the country are visible for miles. The towns and villages seated in the plains, people on foot and people on horseback can be seen at a great distance, and have more the air of light, life, and activity, than many parts of the Boozie country, where the sombre gloom of immense forests conceals all such things. The large town of Du Quirlelah lay on our right, in the bosom of some small hills. It lay on our right; but from our elevated position, it might well be said to lie under us. Going on, we descried a long, whitish border, raised a little above the height of a gentle slope. On drawing near, it proved to be the top of the south-western wall of Musardu. We fired our muskets, and entered the town. We were led up a street, or narrow lane, that brought us into

the square in which the mosque was situated. Here
were gathered the king, Vomfeedolla, and the principal
men of the town, to receive us. My Mandingo friends
from Mohammadu opened the civilities of introduction
with an elaborate speech; stating where I had come
from, and for what I had come; the power, learning,
and wealth of the Tibbabues.

"King Vomfeedolla in appearance has a mild,
gentle countenance. His features would please those
who are fond of a straight nose, broad forehead, thin
lips, large and intelligent eyes, and an oval chin.
Like all the Mandingoes, his skin is a smooth, glossy
black. In stature he is rather below the general
towering height of this tribe. He does not possess
the fiery energy of his royal Boozie brother, Dowilnyah, who, though many years his senior, far excels
him in that respect.

"In all councils Vomfeedolla seems to be entirely
a listener, and to be directed and influenced by the
older members of the royal family. He is said to be
a great warrior; but the evidences around Musardu
prove that if he is, he must belong to the unfortunate
class of that profession.

"The usual apparel or dress of the Mandingoes
consists of four pieces—two pieces as a shirt and vest,
and one large coat or toga worn over all; one pair of
Turkish-shaped trowsers coming a little below the
knees : sandals for the feet, which are sometimes
beautifully worked; and a three-cornered cap for the
head. These articles, made and worn as a Mandingo
only can make and wear them, leave nothing to be
desired, either as to taste or utility. This is said so

far as the men are concerned. But I must deplore a fashion observed by the women, in wrapping up their faces and bodies in a manner truly ungraceful, and unhealthy, too.

"Musardu is an exceedingly healthy place; there was not one prostrate, sickly person in the town. There is, however, a disease which sometimes attacks individuals in a peculiar way; it is an affection of the throat, causing a protuberance almost similar to what is called the 'king's evil.' I inquired the cause, and they imputed it to something that impregnates the water during the height of the dry season, being the time when it mostly seizes persons.

"The atmosphere of Musardu is very dry, and had a very favorable effect upon my watches, which were declared at Monrovia to be out of order ; but as soon as I reached Musardu, every one of them began to tick away in a clear and ringing manner.

"Musardu, the capital of the Western Mandingoes, is in latitude 8 deg. 27 min. 11 sec. N., longitude 8 deg. 24 min. 30 sec. W.; it is elevated two thousand feet above the level of the sea, and is situated amid gentle hills and slopes. North and north-east two very high hills tower above the rest several hundred feet. The population is between seven and eight thousand."

On page 129 of this volume, will be found a fac simile, with a translation of a letter from the King of Musardu to the President of Liberia, which was brought by Mr. Anderson on his return from the exploration.

But interesting and important as is the condition of the Mandingoes, the Fellatahs or Foulahs are perhaps an even more important element in connection with any well directed general Missionary effort in West Africa.

Bishop Payne has lately furnished us with the following extracts regarding them, from "Notes on Northern Africa, the Sahara, and Soudan, by Wm. B. Hodgson, late Consul of the United States near the Regency of Tunis."

FOULAHS AND FELLATAHS.

"Throughout the whole extent of Nigritia, or Negro-land, the Foulahs undoubtedly occupy pre-eminence. They are found spread over a vast geographic region of 28 to 30 deg. in longitude—1,500 miles, and 7 to 10 deg. in latitude, or 500 miles.

"They extend from the Atlantic Ocean, from the mouth of the Senegal and Senegambia on the west, to the Kingdoms of Bornou and Mandara on the east; from the Desert of Sahara on the north, to the mountains of Guinea or Kong on the south. This wide superficies contains more then 700,000 square miles, which is equal to the fourth part of Europe, and a tenth part of the immense continent of Africa. Compared with the United States these parallels of longitude would extend from Maine to Missouri. What may be the Foulah population spread over this region it is impossible to approximate. But the low estimate of three inhabitants to the square mile would give a population of two millions. In the wide extent of this vast region, they are found under the various but similar names of Fellans, Felany, Foulony, Fellatah, Fellatiyah, and Peuls. By linguistic analogies, it was discovered by Adelung, the German philologer, that these widely-separated tribes were one people. In Senegambia and regions adjacent, the Foulahs have formed four principal States, called Fouta-Toro (from Phut?), Fouta-Bondon, Fouta-Djallon, and Fouladon. These States are governed by an elective chief called *Almamy* (el-Imam). He may be termed the President of an oligarchic council. In other negro countries, where these nomadic tribes have introduced themselves, they pay tribute to the chiefs of the country for the lands which they occupy under a certain feudal dependence. In this political relation they are found on all the Atlantic coast (?) from the River Sierra Leone, along the Grain, Ivory, and Gold Coast, to the Niger. On the Senegal they are found among the Serracolets or Sereres, and eastward to Massina. At Jennet, Caillé discovered that they had seized the power of the State, and were defending themselves against the Sergoo Tuaricks to the north, and the Bambara negroes to the south. On the western coast they thus live, mingled with the Jaloofs, Mandingoes and Sousons.[1] On the Niger, and in Soudan they occupy or have conquered the Kingdoms of Yarriba, Nuffee, Haousa and others.

"The Foulahs are *not* negroes. They differ essentially from the negro race in all the characteristics which are marked by physical anthropology. They

[1] From their features I should judge that the *Vyes* around Cape Mount must belong to the Foulah family.   J. P.

may be said to occupy the intermediate space betwixt the Arab and Negro. All travellers concur in representing them as a distinct race in moral as in physical traits. To their color the various terms of *bronze*, *copper*, *reddish*, and sometimes *white*, have been applied. They concur also in the report that the Foulahs of every region represent themselves to be *white* men. Mungo Park's description of them does not vary much from that of all subsequent travellers; and this is substantially repeated in Schön and Crowther's Journal of the Niger Expedition in 1841. They say: ' The Foulahs are chiefly of a tawny complexion, with silky hair and pleasing features.' . . . .

" The Foulahs are a warlike race of shepherds, and within this century they have established a political organization ; subjugated a large portion of Soudan ; and founded Sokatoo, the capital of their empire. Clapperton says that this town, which was built in 1805 by Danfodio, the prophet, and the first political and military chief of the Foulahs, was the most populous which he had seen in Central Africa.

" The Foulahs are rigid Mohammedans, and according to the report of Mollieu, the French traveller, they are animated by a strong zeal for proselytism. They are the Missionaries of Islam among the pagan negro tribes. Where they have conquered they have forced the adoption of the Koran by the sword ; and while pursuing their pastoral occupation, they become schoolmasters, *maalins*—and thus propagate the doctrines and precepts of Islam."

It even seems probable that the pre-occupation of the field by Mohammedanism may prove a help rather than a hindrance to the spread of Christianity.

Professor Blyden writes : "All careful and candid observers agree that the influence of Islam in Central and West Africa has been, upon the whole, of a most salutary character. As an eliminatory and subversive agency, it has displaced or unsettled nothing as good as itself. If it has introduced superstitions, it has expelled superstitions far more mischievous and degrading. And it is not wonderful if, in succeeding to a debasing heathenism, it has in many respects made compromises, so as occasionally to present a barren hybrid character. But what *is* surprising is that a religion quietly introduced from a foreign country, with so few of the outward agencies of civilization, should not in process of time have been altogether absorbed by the superstitions and manners of barbarous pagans. But not only has it not been absorbed, it has introduced large modifications in the views and practices even of those who have but a vague conception of its teachings. Mungo Park, in his travels seventy years ago, everywhere remarked the contrast between the pagan and the Mohammedan tribes of interior Africa."

Mr. Hodgson, whom we have already quoted, writes in a similar strain regarding the Mohammedanism among the Foulahs :

"Wherever the Foulah has wandered, the pagan idolatry of the negro has been overthrown ; the barbarous *fetish* and gree-gree have been abandoned : anthrophagy and cannibalism have been suppressed, and the horrible sacrifice of human beings to propitiate the monstrous gods of the negro barbarian, has been supplanted by the worship of the true GOD.

"Thus the Foulahs are now exercising a powerful influence upon the moral and social condition of Central Africa. I do not doubt that they are to be the great instruments in the future civilization of Africa.

"In Central Africa, education and religious instruction are entirely in the hands of the Mohammedans.

"*The Koran has introduced its letters where it has been adopted, as the Bible from Rome has substituted its letters for the alphabets of Europe.* Let not the humanizing influence of the Koran upon the fetishes, greegrees, and human sacrifices of pagan, homicidal Africa be deprecated. It will bring up the civilization of the barbarous negro races to a certain degree of civilization, and thus it will concur with Christianity, which is now invading Africa from the West, in suppressing their inhuman practices. The *Arabic Bible* is eagerly sought. Let therefore the Gospel be disseminated in *Arabic characters,* into whatever languages the pious zeal of Missionaries may be able to translate it, since Arabic letters have for centuries been introduced into Africa and have become familiarized by use.

"On this subject Sir Powel Buxton says: 'There are points in the Mohammedan faith which we may turn to account in attempting to introduce better instruction. The Mussulmans of the West do not regard Christians with the same horror as those of the East; they seem to be favorably impressed by finding that we acknowledge much of their own sacred history; and with them the names of Abraham and Moses serve

عدة عبيدهم ترتب تحت خسرو و بعضهم رسوله و كلهم صار و بعير و بعضهم اشتروا أنفسه و هؤلاء سبعة
ولد بلد نا وصاحب البلد وقلنا للرسول بعير بيا نسير فإن الملك العزيز أرسلك إلينا هو خضر بمرد يبه
روا ابترس الكارو والملك ليس بلك نا على جا رقد بير قد تغر تا الملك ذهب في بلد نا ابتر ميا وكثير
وهذا لنا في حركة الجيش السمر مرد بيه ذابيع عنا وانصرنا الحذ ديك سيف وملبع به في وانصر
نا بك لشبي انت تعلم انه معدور وانت تحب البنا وما تحبك وملات بالله وبونك وتبعك واعطا
مرد واعطا ان كرامي ملكك وسولك وبتني في صعبو الدثر بسيد افبرالبنايا حبيبي اذا اراد ترسل
علينا لا شك ولا تغير في اصرنا انه بعد ذ فبلك جاء في ملا تنك وبسبب الحب بيني وبينك هو محمد في
كلمنا سابس محمد اذا بلغ رسلك عليه بلغ على اواح اطلم رسوله عليه بلغ عليك وكذا الك العلى اذا
عطانا بصا ابلغ الى محمد واذا اعطاك بصا ابلغ على محمد يا محمد سابس محمد اقى او رزق لاى
ولد في بيد ك اثنير هما انعرب محمد ما لك انت كلتهما لى يا النصارى يا يهود يا اذا اودوا وبيرسل
البنا بلغ على سابس محمد واذا بلغ رسلكم عليه فقد عبدك هو كله فبلصهم وهؤاحب على رد بمرد يبه وكلاما
احد مربلد ذا بعدك او انشاء الله بسبب وسلك وانا ملك الحرب يبذ رحى بلد نا و حرمة هذا البلد عظيم با انت
تكلمه فضل الله على تغير بسيب ذا الك الى بلد نا وهذا لبلد ام القرى واسمه مساد ورى الله التوفيق
او شاء الله لا حول ولا قوة الا بالله العلى العظيم تمت الكلام نيا او اذه في هذا الخط وانا نطلب
منك يا حبيب مرك ما حفظك الله به مع الجيش وغيرها وام رذ كلهم يا معبر صلى محمد وعلى ال محمد

واسمه هذا الخط محمد برتي ليس رلنا علم وما اذا الب العلم وصبى ولكن لكفر العلصا لنا واسم
ابيه ابراهيم واسمه امه عايشة يسر كلمضا مع ايسر ما الله التوفيق

انا كتبته عبد الكريم بيت المال اسم كتبه
جلصيا بيع وابيه سنة سمع وامه مسيكن

بعد هذا رسالة من بلاد الى بلد من بلدنا
ومن الارض ناصر المصيبة والغلاو العبيد
ملك خارج من بلده ... الى بلدنا اسمه
علون سمعوا اسم بلده و ذارك صغير
اكم هو عصر وعطاك الصلاة واعطى
ذراك الى بلده مدير وعلم الله علما
له ثم مات في الجهيد وترك وكد عدذك
خار لله ثم قتل عدوه وترك اخونه
رسس كان ملك بعد هما ود خار
و فيه علينا كثير سوء للذاب مع
لينا وقال يا اهل البلد مساد و في
كم من الكفار و قلنا نعم فال ال
ابي علون سمعوا فيه علته هو
نار قتد ح علد م

والجيش العرم كثير وكلهم فساد اذا رايت بينهم حاجة احد في بلدة واذا رايتهم المعزو الضار اخذ
لنفسه اذ كلام البلد ضربوك واخذ والصراحة لنفسه واذا ويتهم البقري بذا الناس قالوا عطا في بالذين
ان يعطيك العبد اذ قال صاحب الذير ضربه وسبه وقالوا لمن عذ وراى وقال اهل البلد له انه ركا اصبر
لذي فني ماجى بلد فنا مدم وما ولهم معام اخذ فنا الجوع قدمات وولد ناب كثير اوعبد فنا وهربوا الو عدونا لاجل
الجوع وكان غني يكون وفقير وفقير يكون وكثير خوف نا البقر اخذ لنفسهم من غير عوض ولما اعلم
الملك فذا فتنقدا اهل البلد لبيس ما الضمورة معام لهم مورة قولة لهم مورة الجيش لو بلغي قال صاحب
البلد يا اهل البلد احرثوا فلما احرثوا اهل البلد وجد واكعام ومارو البها يم من مم وجرب رو البقر
والغنم والمعزو جاجة ولمعا وكثير ولمط سدنا واهل البلد التي اتت خارج منه فذا اوسع الله عليهم
من كل شي رجع البنام ع الجيش وقطعوا مصلحات بيننا وبين جرنا منهم مسلم وكافر اذا وذو والعسى
الو ذاو هما الي ارضهم اخذ واشاء في بلد نارى ما هرف ا المولنا وولدنا وزوجتنا وجيرنا وعبيد نا
وقالوا صاحب البلد وملط اهل البلد ونق كا ورومع اكحبه قالوا يا اهل البلد ما ينظر في الملك وجيشه
مبتركة اب وكلما فاربه لم يبقعا ولم يرد كالا هدم البلد ولما جاء فا انى ا قتل للمسلمين لا سلام
وذا الكمة برو لم يكر شي مفتلا الا مسلم ولم وبكر شي عبيد ا الا مسلم ولم يكر بكر معظير الا فمسلم
وصار الكفا في ان مرمصيبة الجيش قال الكفا لذا يا اهل المسلمين فذ جاء كم نصر ينصر كم علينا وهو
استن ف اء امر الكفار للمسلمين وليس كا الا ي عجز الملك على الكفر بالقتل واثا على ملك ع سبع سنة والملك
مسلم وراهل الجيس كلهم كافرا ة قليل وليس ا كذ الا اخاي منهم اة فالوا اهل الجيش قبر يوب جير الناس
في ملك فنا من غني ما الى البيس ابكر الا واحدا واثنيزا و ثلاث ت عدة واكمر ويكور وفقد
خسدا واهل البلد كثيرة بعد ذك الا الله وملك

السلام ع شي كة

بسم الله الرحمن الرحيم صلى الله على سيدنا محمد هذا رسالة من بلاد الى بلد من بلدنا
الى بلدكم واسمه بلد تا مساد وي وانكر هكم ماكان في الارض هنا هذ المصيبة والغلاء والعبيد
والجوع والفقر وكان الغني بسبب الجيش وكان الملك خارج من بلده كله الى بلدنا اسمه
ابراهيم سر واسمه شر سر سر واسمه علو سر واسم بلده ودار مذبر
وابنه سفر الى بلد كم حينئذ كان ملك في بلدكم هو عصر وعمال المراة واعطى
اهل البلد كلهم جميع المال كثيرا ورجع الى بلده الى بلده مذبر وعلم الله علما
كثير اعطى الله ولذ كثير وملكا عظيم وفتل الله ثم مات في الجهد وترك وكذ عذر
نسع ذكر واسمه كبير هم عبد الله وفتل كان ار الله ثم فتل عدو وترك اخونه
ابراهيم المد كوري او الاكلام ابراهيم سر كان ملك بعد هما ود خارج
بلد هذا ت يوم يغار ثلت لها اسم اليوم د خار عليه علينا كثير سوء للاداب مع
الجيش العرم مر عار ورد خار في المصلحات لبنا وفار يا اهل البلد مساد وي واني
قد جاني مع الجيش ليقتلوا كل مد كار حو يكم مر الكفار و قلنا نعم فار اني
الملك اني ار الكفار قد حضر كم فار نا ار ايد ابي علو سر واخ اف هو
والمسلمير وفا انا فتك حد علي ه

بسم الله الرحمن الرحيم صلى الله على سيدنا م
الى بلد كم واسم بلد تا مساد وي وانظر كم ماكا
والجوع والبغر وكل مر بسيب الجيش و كا واله
ابراهيم سسر واسرامه شر سسر واسم ابييه
وابنه سعر الى بلد كم حيينذ كا وملك مع بلد
اهل البلد كلهم اجمعين المال كثير و رجع الى
كثير اعطى الله ولذ اكثير وملكا عظيم و قتل ا
نسع ذكر واسم كبير هم عبد الله وقتل كا
ابراهيم المذ كور مع اوا العكلام ابراهيم
بلد ناذات يوم يغال نلت لها اسم اليوم مذ
الجيش العرم مر عا مرود خلج المصلحات :
فذ جانم مع الجيش ليقتلوا كلا مركا رحو
الملك في او العكعا و قذ يضر كم وانا اوا اب
خسد اهل الملك ك

to recommend our holy books. We may make common cause with them, also, in Africa, in our common abhorrence of the bloody rites and sacrifices of the pagans.' "

X.

A LETTER FROM THE KING OF MUSADU.

THE following is a translation with an exact fac-simile, printed from photographic relief plates, of a letter from the King of Musādu to the President of Liberia, written in Arabic, by a young Mandingo, and sent from the capital of the country, two hundred miles northeast of Monrovia. Mr. Benjamin Anderson was the bearer of this letter. The translation is by Rev. Dr. Blyden. The original letter is in the possession of H. M. Schieffelin, New York.

In the name of God, the merciful, the compassion-ate. O God! bless our lord Mohammad and save him. This letter is from towns unto a town—from our town to your town: the name of our town is *Masādu*[1] (accent on the second syllable) that you may see what misfortunes have happened to our country, and carnage and slavery and hunger and poverty, and every injury, on account of the army.

The king came forth from his town to our town; his name is Ibrahima Sisi, and his mother's name Shiri

[1] Thus spelled in the MS. ; sometimes it is written *Misādu* and sometimes *Musādu*.

6*

Sisi, and his father's name Mulul Sisi, and the name of his town and place of residence is Medina.[1] His father travelled to your country (*i. e.* Mesurado). At that time there was a king in your country; his name was Amara. He gave to this king a wife, and gave to all the people of the country plenty of money; then he returned to his town and to his residence Medina (God knows all things). God gave him many children and a large kingdom, and he fought for God, and God killed him and he died in war. He left nine male children. The name of the eldest was Abdallah. He fought against the infidels (Kafirs) for God, and the enemy slew him, and he left his brother Ibrahima above mentioned. Now Ibrahima is king after them. He entered our town on a certain Tuesday. On that day he came to us with horses and a numerous, overwhelming and impudent army, and entered upon an agreement with us and said, "O ye people of the town of Masādu, I have come with my army to fight against all those around you who are infidels or pagans." And we said, "Very well." And the king said, "I see that the pagans have injured you, and I have seen my father, Mulul Sisi, and my brother, Abdallah, that they fought for God and the Muslims, and I said I will humble them in battle, and there shall be no honor that a child should have his origin from the town of his parents." And the people of the town said, "Preserve thou our

[1] This is a very extensive Muslim city, surrounded with mud walls, about two days' journey east of Misādu. Ibrahima, who presides over it, is an enterprising and powerful young Mussulman chief, having a large army, consisting of infantry and a cavalry of a thousand horse. He is not a very scrupulous Muslim, however, as appears from the MS.

honor, do not cause defilement or injury in our town."
He said, " Very well ; for this army will not injure anything except what I command it." And the people
said, "Do what pleases thee, for this town is thine."
And the King said, " I am going forth from our town
that I may fight their towns who troubled you, and
fight the Kafirs around you. Have you not heard
the saying of the prophet (God bless him), I command that you fight men until they say there is no
God but God. And they said, "Yes, we have
heard it, and we know it." And they said, "Do
what thou hast said." And when he perceived
that the people of the town were pleased with
his speech, he went with his numerous and arro-
gant army and fought against the people of a town
called Baghna, and returned to us and entered our
walled town and our houses. When he perceived
that the believers had cut off relations between themselves and the pagans, and had destroyed all marriage
connections between them, and had destroyed friendship, he said to the leaders of the slaves (the number
of the leaders of the slaves was nine), " Fight, do not
let (the enemy) gather one with another until they
become numerous. Gather yourselves together, and
go around them and attack them on all sides. Every
one who attempts to escape, capture for us, keep him
or kill him. I will sit in the capital of the country,
Masadu, with numerous boys and the large army.

And when he (the king) saw fowls in the town (Masadu) he took them, or goats or sheep or women, he
took them for himself. And when he saw cows in the
possession of any one he said, " Give them to me for

the sake of religion ; I will give you slaves." When
he said, " companion of the faith " he struck them and
captured them, and he said, " These are the enemies
of my father." And the people of the town said to
him, " Desist, there is not in our town any money or
food. Hunger has taken possession of us, and many
of our children and slaves have either died or fled to
our enemies on account of hunger ; and all our rich
men have become poor, and the poor have become
numerous. Slaves have taken our female children to
themselves without compensation." And when the
king perceived the poverty of the people of the town,
that they had neither money nor food nor power, he
returned with his army to his town (Medina).

The chief of the town (Masādu) then said, "O ye
people of the town, plant, plant." And when the people of the town planted, they found food and money
and calves from the pasture, and cows and sheep and
goats and fowls and an abundance of food. And
when he (Ibrahima) heard that God had produced for
the people of the town whom he had abandoned, a
greater abundance of everything, he returned to us
with the army, and broke the agreement between us
and our neighbors, both Muslims and Pagans. And
when they desired the journey to their home and to
their country, they took from us the best in our town
and our houses, our goods and our children and our
wives and our neighbors and our slaves; and they
said, " When we have removed their slaves and their
children and their wives, they shall sweat with us."

And when we heard this saying from them, the
chief and king of the town, Fanfi Doreh, with his

companions said, "O ye people of the town, do ye see the king and his army, how all that he has said he does not do it, and he does not desire it, except the destruction of the town. When he came he said, "I will fight for the Muslims," but he has had no one to fight against except Muslims, and there are no slaves except Muslims, and there are no poor except Muslims. The Kafirs have escaped from the calamities of the army. And say the Kafirs to us, "O ye Muslim people, help came to you to assist you against us." And this was a taunt from the Pagans to the Muslims. This was the king's weakness before the Kafirs. And we were in this condition for seven years. The king was a Muslim and all the people of his army were Kafirs except a few. And there was not one of the people of the town but feared when it was said, " The army is on the road." Men fled from their misfortunes. And all the wealthy people in our town had not anything left in their hands except one or two or three slaves; all were poor on account of the army, and we spurned them (the army); and the people of the town lost many things, and none but God can number them; and our king, whose name is Fanfi Doreh, lost sixty slaves.

On a certain day we saw the people of the army, and they entered a town below us toward the west, and the name of the town was Yusumudu. They attacked it until they spoiled the houses and broke down the walls and made the farms to suffer; and they wasted another town below us on the west; the name of this town is Khulila. And when they returned to their town, some came to our town (Jilila),

and they killed in it one hundred and eighty sheep
and goats, and the people of that town were Muslims.
For this reason the people of our town refused their
friendship, reproached them, and did not say " Peace "
to them. We thought that they were helpers of the
religion of Mohammad, but they were not helpers of
Islam, but they destroyed the religion of Islam.
They were disobedient to God and followed Satan ;
and therefore I take refuge in God [1] from their
punishment and their wickedness. May God preserve
us from them and from the evil of many visits from
them. They reviled the holy priest of the town, and
assaulted him, taking his garment from his loins and
even his cap from his head, and they outraged him
and dragged him over the ground, and they greatly
damaged him with their feet ; his name is Salihu
Shereef. They laid waste and destroyed all the
treasures of the country. And no one knows the
number of their evil deeds, and how to describe them,
but God.

When they entered the town they made the greater
portion of the inhabitants of the town poor and destitute and vile, even the learned men became poor. If
it had been known to us what they would do to us
before it took place, we should certainly have driven
them away, and they would not have entered. Says
Hariri, in the Makamot, " We said they are weak and
we are weak ; they are men and we are men " [2] .   .   .
They will not ever enter into our town. Verily God
is mighty, and verily there is a refuge in God, and

[1] Koranic form for introducing deprecatory invocations.—*Trans.*
[2] MS. not intelligible here.

every man should seek to serve God in everything.

And, during this state of things, we learned on a
certain day, that there was a messenger on the path
from Durukoro [1] to us, from a place on the west and
its environs, and we said, " Praise be to God for that.
This is our wish and our ardent desire." The army
took from our town seven men, and selected the best
of them, and some of their slaves, fifty belonging to
some and under fifty belonging to others. Seven
children of our town and the Iman saved themselves
by flight. We said to the messenger, Ben Anderson,
say to the king who sent thee to us, as follows : " We
have seen thy messenger. Our town is not in its
former condition. The king (Ibrahima) has troubled
us. The army entered into our town and threw us
into confusion. Assist us with iron and sword, and
with everything. Thou knowest that he has been a
help. Thou lovest us and we love thee, and our
refuge is in God and in thee, and in thy assistance
and thy companionship. Give us whatever is in thy
kingdom. Thy messenger has seen us in affliction on
account of the war which has come to us. O my
friend, when thou desirest to travel to us do not
doubt or be troubled on account of our affairs. Come
without doubt on account of the love between us and
thee.

There is Mohammed, called in our language, " Sabsu," [2] when thy messenger reaches to him he reaches
to us, and when our messenger reaches to him he
reaches to thee ; and likewise presents from thee to me

---

[1] Monrovia.   [2] Momoru Sau, King of Boporo.

may come through Mohammad, and presents from me to thee by the same means.

Oh, Mohammad Sabsu,[1] I visit thee, but thou dost not visit me, for my two children are with thee (in thy hand), viz., Nafaribu Mohammad and Maliki, thou keepest them for me.

Oh, Christians and Jews,[2] when ye desire to send to us, send to Mohammad Sabsu, and when your messages reach him, his servant Kuhi will forward them, for he loves us; and all that you desire from our town you will find, if it please God, according to your letter. I am king of the army in our town, the protector of this large town. This town is the mother of the country—the name is Masàdu. Success is from God, if it please God. There is no strength or power but in God, the exalted, the mighty. The word is finished which I wished in this letter, and I pray for thee, O friend, that God may keep thee from the army and all its mischiefs. Peace upon Mohammad and the family of Mohammad.

The name of the writer of this book is Mohammad Barta. I have no learning—I seek learning. I am but a boy, but I think that there are learned men among us. The name of his father is Ibrahima, and of his mother Ayesha. Success is from God.

[1] The King of Masàdu here addresses the King of Boporo, as Mr. Anderson had to pass through his town going and coming.

[2] The Mandingoes regard the Liberians as composed of Christians and Jews.

EXTRACTS

FROM N. Y. STATE COLONIZATION JOURNAL, APRIL, 1871.

ADDRESS BY REV. A. CRUMMELL,

DELIVERED AT MONROVIA, LIBERIA, IN JULY, 1870.

WE have received a copy of an address, delivered in July last at Monrovia, by the Rev. Alexander Crummell, a missionary of the Episcopal church at Caldwell, Liberia. Mr. Crummell is known to many of our readers as the son of a native African, brought as a slave from a point within 100 miles of Monrovia. The son was born in Brooklyn, educated in part at a public school in New York, then at the Oneida Institute, near Utica, and was subsequently a member of Queens College at the University of Cambridge, where he received his bachelor's degree. He was for some time a professor in Liberia College. He is a man eminent for piety and learning and ardent devotion to the elevation of his race. We give a few extracts from the address, and did our space permit, would be happy to lay it in full before our readers.

One mistake of the people of Liberia, has been neglect of our native population. . . . We have been guilty of a neglect which has carried with it harm to the aborigines, and at the same time visited grievous wrong upon ourselves.

No native king has ever had sent to him by the government a teacher to educate his children and his people. No sons of princes have been brought from our native tribes to be educated by the government. . . . No native kings or head men have ever been invited to sit as advisers or senators in our legislature, to represent their tribes and to show them the advantage of civilized and responsible government.

The native man has not only physical capacity, but he has also the habit of labor. He is a worker. . . . The native African does work, and that most gladly, up to the level of his cultivation and his needs ; not, indeed, I grant you, up to the civilized man's needs, for he is a barbarian. He does not work for a brick house, for carpets and chairs, for books and pictures. He has not reached the point of civilization which requires such things. Neither did Mr. Carlyle's grandfathers when Cæsar came to Britain.

Have faith in the native. You have trusted him,—trusted him to nurse your children ; trusted him with your goods in trading ; trusted your life in his hands in fragile canoes ; trusted yourself unprotected in his sequestered native villages. Go now to a further length, trust him as a man fitted to

"Move and act
In all the correspondencies of nature."

Fellow-citizens ! whether willing or unwilling ; whether from necessity or at the urgent call of Christian duty, we must educate and elevate our native population. Here we are a feeble folk in the midst of their multitudes. If we neglect them, then they will surely drag us down to their rude condition and their deadly superstitions, and our children at some future day will have cast aside the habiliments of civilized life, and lost the fine harmonies and the grand thoughts of the English tongue.

In their poverty, the New York State Colonization Society desires to uphold the hands of this "feeble folk" in efforts to extend civilization and Christianity to the multitudes around them.

THE GIBBEE COUNTRY, LIBERIA.

A line of broken mountains near the coast, leaves Liberia without navigable streams, while supplying it with inexhaustible water-power.

The earliest settlement of the colony of Liberia was at Cape Messurado, near the mouth of the St. Paul's river, in 1821.

Twelve years afterward a second point on the coast was selected for a settlement, sixty miles south-east of Cape Messurado, at the mouth of the St. John's river, in Grand Bassa.

Neither of the rivers are navigable for more than ten or twelve miles from the sea, as they rush down over many rapids from the interior.

Halfway between the two rivers mentioned, a large stream empties into the ocean, called the Junk river, consisting of two principal branches—the Red Junk, draining the coast for twenty miles to the north-west, and the Farmington river, breaking through the mountain chain from the east. As one sails along the coast the mountain chain no where seems so bold and near at hand as at the Junk river.

The Bassa native tribe inhabits the coast from the Junk river for nearly 100 miles south-east, extending 70 miles to the interior.

We received last summer from Rev. T. E. Dillon, a Presbyterian missionary at Marshall, near the mouth of the Junk river, an account of a journey he had just made to explore its course, and present our readers with the following extracts:

Last March I visited the Gibbee, a populous country east of Marshall, on the Farmington river, and about 100 miles from its mouth. A direct line, however, would greatly lessen the distance, as the road usually travelled follows the course of the river, which winds about, first in a zig-zag, and then in a curvilinear manner. Five rapids, situated from 12 to 20 miles apart, prevent ascending this river in a single canoe, but the use of four canoes, one between each pair of rapids, and a short walk around each fall, would obviate the difficulty of ascending it.

The Gibbee people are a branch of the Bassa family, which spreads over one-half of the republic on the coast, and in the interior beyond our limits. After leaving Mount Olivet, a missionary station of the M. E. church, about 15 miles from the sea, I reached the Gibbee, after four full days' walk through an uninhabited country, with all varieties of soil and numerous streams of the purest water. (March is at the close of a long dry season.)

I regret my inability to give a complete and connected statement of all I saw and heard before, and especially after reaching the Gibbee country.

I preached while out there as often as opportunity offered. Sometimes, for want of room, I have stood out, on a beautiful moonlight night, and preached to a whole town consisting of five hundred souls, who crowded around me, some, it may be, to be taught the truth, but the most from curiosity, for it was a novelty to all, many of whom had never before seen an American.

I usually spent a portion of every day instructing them from a small primer I had taken along for the purpose, and in rehearsing simple stories from the Bible, and was agreeably surprised to witness the remarkable aptitude in learning they evinced—some quite learning the alphabet.

There are some curiosities in this country, viz. : a large stone cavern and some rocks, chiefly remarkable for their form and size, which lie at the basis of the Bee, the highest peak of a chain of mountains and hills which describe a circle of 20 miles in diameter, enclosing a basin of the very richest soil, ever receiving increased richness from the surrounding mountain sides. This peak, the Bee, is seen from Cape Messurado, from Careysburgh, from Marshall, and from the sea, being over 3,000 feet high.

When on the western side of the top of the mountain we have an open level plot, from which is afforded a panoramic view of all the country toward the sea. I ascended the mountain April 5th, about 3 p. m., and as I beheld at one view, Junk mountain to the south-west, Careysburgh and Monrovia to the west, the Boporo mountains toward the north, dozens of hills and cones, an immense wilderness and a score or more of native villages lying below the mountains, I thought surely it was the most sublime prospect that ever greeted my eyes! The mountain is covered with large trees, such as are common to this country ; only a few of them camwood trees, but the best of building timbers can be procured here, and clay for brick-making. The stones are chiefly flint, in all stages of decomposition. There is some iron ore, but I saw no signs of gold. The elevation of this ridge and the tremendous precipice that bounds it on the west, prevent access by invaders, and the inhabitants of the valley boast that they have never been whipped.

The east side is less broken, and here are to be seen the greatest specimens of large rocks, which seem, by some violent cause, to have been hurled from the top and sides of the mountain. One of these is a large rocking stone, resting on a very narrow base, apparently almost on nothing, fully 60 feet long and 20 feet high, and looking very dangerous. On the south-eastern side of the mountain peak, about 40 feet above its base, there is a large cavern, formed chiefly by three huge rocks. It is reached through a stony pathway, rocks on either hand towering far overhead. It is entered through an aperture seven-and-a-half feet by four feet, and consists of two apartments, the first 52 feet, and the second apartment 48 feet in length, by ten feet in width. The rocks are calcareous flint, porous, and usually full of water ; and being exceedingly brittle, I considered it dangerous to go under them, as it is possible for them to fall in when well saturated with water. On a clear day the cavern has sufficient light for all ordinary purposes. It is occupied by vampires in abundance, and these rocks are the god of the Gibbee people. They make continual offerings of old broken pipes, bowls, tobacco, etc., and through it professedly they achieve all their victories over their enemies in war, etc. To it they offer their devotions or prayers, and seldom a day passes that these rocks are not visited by some one of the natives, either to make sacrifices, or to pray to this rock.

I am persuaded that much good could be done among this people, by introducing schools among them. They are numerous, and are willing to be taught. I tried, but in vain, to enumerate the children. They are not, indeed, innumerable, but they are very numerous.

Nawvlee's Town is the capital, and contains nearly one hundred houses and five hundred people, in addition to a great number of half towns scattered over the country for five or six miles from the capital. There are several towns in Gibbee nearly as populous as Nawvlee's. Towns in that region are usually large, and contain more children than towns near our settlements. Here in Liberia the boys are put out among the Liberian settlers, to be employed in labor or to learn to speak English. But in the Gibbee country it is not unusual to see, of a moonlight evening, from 75 to 100 playing in the open yards or in the streets of the town.

A missionary sent there should be allowed a competent outfit of necessaries, to avoid the necessity of visiting or sending to the settlements often. He should also be supplied with two or three good families, themselves as missionaries, teachers, helpers, etc.

In another letter, dated December 30th, 1870, just received, Mr. Dillon writes :

When in the Gibbee country, I was within twenty miles of

George L. Seymour's mission of 1859, among the Pessy people.[1] The station was called Paynville, the native name being Darpeh.

The king of that country sends down every year urging the government to send them a missionary, and to give them a school.

I would willingly go out there, if the Board would allow, and give me suitable help. I would desire a few persons, as teachers, to accompany me and co-operate with me in the work. I think I would be willing to spend my life among them.

DONATIONS FOR SUPPORT OF SCHOOLS.

There are whole tribes of native Pagans in Liberia, who are included in the half million often spoken of as constituting a part of that republic who to this very day never had a school-house opened for their children. Among them polygamy prevails. Slaves are held and bought and sold; even cannibalism is practiced in some instances. Fifty years have passed since Liberia was founded, and the cry of the natives for schools has been coming over the water, but as to most of the tribes it has been in vain.

Convinced that without schools Liberia and its surrounding population will not be elevated, this Society desires to answer the calls so loud and urgent. *One hundred and twenty-five* dollars pledged by a Sabbath-school, or an individual, will keep one school for a year, in which from fifteen to twenty children can be taught to read the word of God.

[1] Mr. Seymour was a Presbyterian missionary. While exploring further interiorward, he was wounded, and died from the effects, and his mission was thus ended.

Truth will thus help to cast out diabolical superstitions, and reform evil institutions.

Pledges for support of a school are earnestly solicited.

SCHOOLS IN AFRICA.

Many letters from Ashmun, the preserver of Liberia, were laden with appeals for schools and education for the native tribes in Liberia forty years ago. Were he alive, and again looking out from Cape Messuradu, the same appeals would come with increasing earnestness.

Two years ago the New York State Colonization Society began an effort to supply a part of the great field. The results have fallen far below their wishes, and Africa's needs. Something has been secured. Fourteen schools have been set in operation; a large supply of school-books and needful school apparatus sent out and distributed; many teachers were found to be ready, well recommended, to teach primary schools.

By the generous liberality of a friend in Great Britain, means have been furnished to commence a Manual Labor Institute, for the training of a higher class of teachers, and especially looking to lay hold of that most interesting element of native population, which, by commerce, brings the interior Mohammedan population into regular communication with Liberia. Measures are now under way to have such a school opened on the path from Monrovia to Boporo and Misadu.

We append extracts from two or three reports recently received from teachers along eighty miles of the coast.

Each of their schools is supported for a year for $125. One of these teachers had *fourteen native* boys living in her family, and instructed for this mere pittance.

Thirty other schools could at once be opened under Christian teachers, at no greater expense.

A native prince now in this city, from the large Bassa tribe in Liberia, stated in Dr. Garnet's church that not a school-house had been given to his tribe by the people of Liberia in forty years. He asks that his people may have light.

Mrs. Emma A. Diggs, in her report of the school at Robertsport, in August, states the roll at thirty-three scholars; eighteen male and fifteen female.

On Sabbath these chiefly attended a Sunday-school taught by Rev. Mr. MacMillan, a candidate for the ministry, and Mrs. Diggs gathered a few around the water-side. She asks for two or three catechisms. Three persons had recently joined the church.

Mrs. Henry Tyler, in her report at the close of the fourth quarter, Dec. 27th, says:

The number of different scholars during the year has been fifty-three; the average attendance has been twenty-three. The scholars have made good progress in the different studies, especially in spelling, reading, writing and arithmetic.

Mrs. Z. A. King, who teaches in a native village called Gozimbostown, reports for the two quarters from July to December, 1870, eight males and two females, who averaged an attendance of fifty-five days each, out of sixty days that school was open; three

7

attended every day; seven fifty days each. The other lads came in the last three weeks, and attended regularly.

Mrs. King writes:

These children have improved very much, being natives. Some of them have spelled through, and read through, Wilson's Spelling-book, and are also nearly through the smaller Catechism. I had a great deal of trouble, at first, to get them to understand or give attention, but since they have begun to understand, we are encouraged to expect more will be brought into the school in the ensuing year.

Mrs. H. A. Stephen, who taught the Macedonia school in a native village of Day people and Congoes, several miles north of Clay Ashland, reports, Dec. 31, 1870, fourteen males and seven females in her school.

She writes:

I have fourteen of these children living with me in my family, and they are all very anxious to learn, indeed. They spell and read well for the time that they have been with me. I believe the blessing of God has been with us, though we have had a great deal of trouble this year. Since these children are doing so well at learning their books, the natives are very anxious for this school to be continued.

I am pleased to inform you that I have a very fine Sabbath-school. There are a goodly number of adult natives attending it sometimes, and also there are several families of Congoes, who have moved out to my station; they and their children attend the Sabbath-school.

Mrs. E. R. C. Britton, teacher at Harrisburg, reports, under date of November 25:

Sir: I forward this report of the first and second quarters of the school I have kept. The whole number of scholars was fifteen. Of them thirteen were boys—two were girls. All but two were children of colonists. All of these scholars but two commenced with the alphabet. Considering the disadvantage of not having suitable books, the advancement of the scholars was satisfactory.

JACOB W. VONBRUNN.

The arrival of Mr. Vonbrunn by the ship Golconda realizes to us one trophy of missionary labor in Africa.

Mr. Vonbrunn is the son of a subordinate king of the Grand Bassa people, a native tribe extending along the coast of Liberia, from near Monrovia to Grand Colo, 100 miles, and into the interior 90 or 100 miles.

When a lad twelve years of age—the American colonists then occupying only one point on the coast of Africa, at Cape Messurado—Vonbrunn was sent to the Cape by his father, from St. John's River, Grand Bassa, to learn "American fash," and to get a smattering of colloquial English, and some ideas of civilization. This was about 1830. There a missionary, who had gone to Africa in response to an earnest appeal of Governor Ashmun for teachers for the colonists and natives, saw the lad, and took him for education.

When the mission became so weakened by death and sickness as to be abandoned, Mr. Kisseling, with consent of the father, took the lad with him to Sierra Leone, where, after a careful training, he was baptized, and became a teacher in the schools for re-captives.

In one of these village schools, in a quiet mountain valley, the writer of this article first saw Vonbrunn in 1840. He was in charge of 400 scholars, of whom 270 were present. The Lancasterian system was used, and the smaller scholars were taught by scholars of more advanced classes.

In 1854, Vonbrunn had returned to his own native town and tribe, in Bassa Liberia, and was employed by Rev. Mr. Clark, a Baptist missionary, as assistant teacher.

His return to his father and tribe had been an occasion of greatest joy to them ; and on the death of the father, the people demanded of him to accept the succession, and become their king. This he resolutely refused ; and finally, to satisfy his scruples, they left their old devil ground, and built a new town near the mission, in which he acted as a magistrate, commissioned by the Liberian government. Were he willing he could now hold the succession to the principal kingship of the whole tribe, but he will not.

During 1869 and 1870, commissioned to preach as a Baptist missionary, he visited many villages and large towns up the St. John's river, in little Bassa, in the Gibbee country, and east of the Coast Range of mountains, and found a universal willingness to hear.

He expressed a desire to visit America in a letter received October, 1870, and arrived in New York by the ship Golconda, February 24th. His object was twofold ; first to enlarge his own mental powers, by the sight of our Christian civilization, institutions, and material prosperity ; and secondly, to bring the wants of his nation before our Christian people, and elicit more aid in the way of schools. He justly remarks that the Liberians are as yet unable to support their own churches or schools, and therefore quite unable to help his people.

Some opposition was made by his people to his coming away, but when assured that he might bring them teachers, they yielded, and are now awaiting his return with hope and anxiety. Shall he carry back assurances of schools and Bibles?

EXPLORATIONS EAST OF LIBERIA.

Stimulated by the liberal aid of one of our retired New York merchants, an active member of the New York State Colonization Society, who had offered to defray the expenses of an exploration toward the river Niger, Benjamin Anderson, a Liberian, left Monrovia February 14, 1868, and overcoming all the schemes of opponents, whether of civilized or uncivilized, Mohammedan or Pagan traders, bravely persevered, till after nine-and-a-half months of vexatious detentions, on Monday, Dec. 27, 1868, he had penetrated to Musadu, a large walled town of the Mandingoes.

He had passed through five tribes—the Day, the Goulah, the Vey, the Condo, or Boson people, the Domar Bonsie, and the Wymar Bonsie tribes. As his estimates and observations show, his journey terminated about 200 miles in a direction nearly northeast of Monrovia.

The accessibility of the interior plateau, and the existence of large tribes of industrious native people, ready and anxious to open commerce, being thus demonstrated, on the return of Anderson, in March, and the publication of his journal to Musadu, interest was awakened, and early in 1870 the Episcopal missionary at Monrovia, planted a mission school at Totoquella, the new capital of the Boson or Condo people, 90 miles north of Monrovia. President Roye had scarcely been inaugurated, before he resolved to explore a more direct road to Musadu ; and in May, 1870, Wm. S. Anderson, one of the largest sugarmakers of Liberia, was commissioned for this purpose. He was supplied with goods for presents to the chiefs and to meet expenses, furnished with forty men well armed as a guard, and authorized to enter into treaties of amity and commerce. His course was on the south-east side of the St. Paul's river, leading him through the Bassa, Pessy and Barline tribes, entirely distinct in language and nationality from those on the north-western side of the river. This journey was quite a success. The show of strength and liberal presents to the chiefs, removed all obstacles, and in eight days Mr. Anderson had penetrated within fifty miles of Musadu.

He was heartily welcomed by tribes who had before been represented as cannibals. He found them dwelling in large walled cities, busily engaged in various industrial pursuits, the fields finely cultivated with growing crops of rice, cotton, corn, and various vegetables. Cotton robes and iron were manufactured extensively, and the people were eager for commercial relations with Liberia. On his return, the presents brought to President Roye from the native chiefs— ivory, cotton robes, bullocks, etc., convinced all the Liberians that a large and lucrative field of commerce, right at their door, had been too long neglected.

We are glad to learn that by order of President Roye, block-houses are, at the present time, being built along a direct path to the Pessy and Barline country, soon, perhaps, to reach Musadu and the Niger river, and open an inviting field for missionary labor.

HELP FOR AN EDUCATION.

C———, LIBERIA, *August* 21, 1871.

Rev. J. B. Pinney, Secretary of the N. Y. State Colonization Society.

SIR : I beg you will excuse the liberty I am taking to write to you, but I am encouraged to apply to you in the hope that you will kindly assist me in the effort I am making to acquire an education. I am a member of the Methodist church, and have endeavored to live a consistent Christian life. I applied to President Roberts in the early part of the year, to receive me in the preparatory department as a beneficiary, but he informed me that he had no funds then with which he could aid me. I am a poor boy, and feel willing to make any reasonable sacrifice to improve my education, that I may be useful in this country. I came to Liberia, a child, with my parents, fifteen years ago. They both soon died, and left me an orphan, and I have had a hard time, with scarcely any opportunity afforded me to improve my mind ; but I neglected no means that I could avail myself of, and now feel more and more the want of a better education ; and if the N. Y. State Colonization Society will aid me, I pledge myself to

the gospel ministry, and will do all in my power
to evangelize the heathen.

A NATIVE TRAVELLER.

On Saturday, the 27th ultimo, there arrived at the
residence of Professor Blyden a young Mandingo
Mussulman, of the name of Lusannu, from Tenkereh,
a populous city lying to the east of Musâdu. He
was introduced to the professor by Famba Sissi,
a Moslem, resident of Vonzowah.

Lusannu, having a roving disposition, left his
father when a boy of ten years of age, and followed
trading caravans or military expeditions. He is now
about twenty-three years old. In his wanderings he
visited Bamako and Yamina, on the Niger. He knows
also Timbo, Jenneh, Hamd-Allahi, and Tangrera.
He has resided at Falabar and Finamisaya. He has
been at the gold-diggings at Buleh. He had not
been so far as Sokoto or Kane, but had frequently
met traders from those places. From Timbuctoo
traders carry rock salt to his native city for sale.
Asses, horses, cows, sheep, etc., are numerous. Tenkereh is about a week's journey to the eastward of
Musâdu, but the people go towards the big water to
trade, which Lusannu describes as not far from
Tenkereh, no doubt the head waters of the Niger. It
is almost certain that the sources of the Niger are
within a few days' journey from Cape Palmas.

Lusannu had no books or manuscripts with him,
though his father is one of the learned Mohammedans.
Having spent all his days in itinerant and warlike

employments, he had not made much proficiency in letters. He recited, however, from memory, with great accuracy and fluency, several chapters from the Koran in Arabic. He describes Tenkereh as five times the size of Monrovia.—*Liberia Register*.

From the Liberia Herald.

We are indebted to Mr. Dennis for calling the attention of our people to the "amicable and politic discretion which should influence their conduct in their intercourse with their native brethren."

It is the policy of the present Administration, which, to the extent of its ability, it has been striving to carry out—to be "energetic in its demonstrations of sympathy towards the aborigines." To treat our aborigines as colonists in other parts of the world have treated the natives of the country in which they settled, would be extremely foolish as well as impolitic.

We are one people. There is not the superiority of one class to another, of one caste to another, of one race to another, which we see in India, New Zealand, and North America. If there is any advantage here, it is on the side of the native. We may have the accident of civilization—but he has the essentials of an uncorrupted and untrammelled manhood.

The position which Mr. Dennis and others have taken lately in relation to a proper policy towards the aborigines, illustrates one valuable result of the discussions which have been going on for the last three or four years on the subject of native incorporation, finding its most eloquent expression in the oration

7*

delivered by Professor Crummell, on the 26th of July
last. And in proportion as a truer conception of our
relations to the tribes around us becomes familiar, a
more liberal and comprehensive sentiment will be
generated, and the republic will advance with surer
and more rapid steps on the road to prosperity and
independence.

THE NEW YORK STATE COLONIZATION SOCIETY.

The objects and aims of the New York State Colonization Society are given in its Constitution, as follows :

" ART. 2. The objects of this Society shall be to colonize, with their own consent, people of color of the
United States on the coast of Africa, and through them
to civilize and Christianize the African tribes ; and, also,
generally to improve the condition of the colored population of our country."

The charter granted by the Legislature of New York
states them as follows :

" SEC. 2. The particular business and objects of the
said Society are to provide the ways and means, and
to manage, appropriate and apply the same, to
colonize, with their own consent, people of color of
the United States on the coast of Africa, and through
them to civilize the African tribes ; and, also, generally
to improve the condition of the colored population of
our country, collecting, receiving, appropriating or
investing funds for purposes of *education* in its various
branches, among people of color of our country, here-
tofore colonized, or hereafter to be colonized in Africa,
and by other measures conducive to the objects of
African colonization."

These have been had in view for the last thirty years. It has never confined its operations simply to removing people of color from this country and placing them in Africa to prepare themselves homes in a tropical forest, but has endeavored to aid them when placed there to elevate themselves, and by there example and efforts to promote Christian civilization among their barbarian neighbors. Most of the emigrants from this country have gone to Liberia very poor and very ignorant. A very large proportion were born and bred in slavery. They were in childhood deprived of opportunities to learn the rudiments of common education, and on their arrival at their new home subjected to a severe acclimating process, and were unable to do much more than prepare homes for their families. With a large majority of the people this still remains the case. Surrounded by, and intermingled with an uncivilized people, they are too poor to maintain schools even for their own children.

In the autumn of 1868 our Corresponding Secretary made an exploration of the whole of Liberia, and found in actual operation less than thirty schools to supply a civilized population of fifteen thousand, and an aboriginal population of several hundred thousand. And these schools were, to a great extent, destitute of books, maps, paper, slates, and all aids to instruction. On his return, this Society immediately sent out a supply of books, slates, pencils, maps, paper and ink, to the value of over $1800, and since then has directed its efforts chiefly to promoting primary education. There is ample encouragement to efforts in this

direction. Every village and every settlement of
colonists is anxious for a school, and the head men of
the native towns for a great distance into the interior,
urgently ask for schools where their children may be
taught the "America man's" language and "fash."
The government of Liberia has, since the visit of our
secretary, enacted laws requiring schools to be
established, but the act is almost a dead letter for the
want of means to carry it into effect. It will be some
years before the people will be able to maintain their
own schools, and until then, if aid is not afforded them
from abroad, a large proportion of their children will
grow up in ignorance. Had this Society the means,
it could at once establish a hundred schools, which,
attended by many thousands of colonists and aboriginal children, would help to prepare a generation to
carry on the work as the capacities of the republic
are developed. The first schools would not be of as
high grade as are our common schools in New York.
Teachers of such schools cannot be obtained. But
there can be obtained on the ground, teachers to keep
schools which would compare with many which, within a quarter of a century, could be found in our new
settlements, taught by young women whose early education was only to read, write and cipher. Such
schools in multitudes of cases elevated themselves;
and by aid of modern school-books their teachers also
educated themselves, and became qualified to teach
branches of learning of which at first they were
profoundly ignorant. Elihu Burritt well said, that to
know how to read is the key to all learning. Such
schools were the germs of the valuable ones which are

now everywhere found, the pride of all our citizens as. well as the safeguards of our institutions. A very small outlay will now maintain such a school, and when one is established, we have a right to expect it to improve and prepare pupils to become teachers of schools of much higher grade.

All remittances for the New York State Colonization Society should be made to ISAAC T. SMITH, Treasurer, at the Metropolitan Savings Bank, No. 123 Third Avenue, or to the Corresponding Secretary, Rev. J. B. PINNEY, Room 42, Bible House.